Praise for *The Wolf at the Door*, also by Michael Hackard

"A powerful book that I think really addresses the issue of why we have to look after the elderly . . . in our communities and throughout the country."
—Cyrus Webb, Conversations LIVE host on Blog Talk Radio

"I really appreciate the fact that [Hackard is] looking out for those who are vulnerable at this particular stage of life. I think we're going to see more and more of these situations as the baby boomer generation continues to get older. Hopefully [Hackard's] book will do a lot of good."
—Drew Mariani, The Drew Mariani Show

"I hope that the listeners of this show. . . heed the steps [made] in the book to protect their elders and protect themselves."
—Sharon Kay, What's the 411? host on WFSK 88.1–Nashville

"A great book for anyone who is concerned about protecting older people. . . . An outstanding, wonderful piece of information for those of you who may be concerned about undue influence and elder financial abuse."
—Chuck Finney, KALW 91.7–San Francisco Public Radio

"I like that the book really breaks it down in terms of giving you steps you can take to prevent something like [elder financial abuse] from happening."
—Simone de Alba, KTXL FOX40–Sacramento

"When I look at this book, *The Wolf at the Door*, it scares me enough to want to do something."
—Carlos Amezcua, KUSI TV–San Diego

"I've read the book. It's a good book. It's a necessary book if you find yourself approaching [an elder financial abuse] situation."
—Steve Pomeranz, The Steve Pomeranz Show

"A super valuable book."
—Mike Finney, KGO 810–San Francisco

"The Wolf at the Door: Undue Influence and Elder Financial Abuse illuminates the way tensions in blended families can lead to hideous inheritance disputes."
—Jane Wollman Rusoff, ThinkAdvisor

"Michael Hackard's book offers a comprehensive look at the dangers of elder financial abuse and the legal steps needed for protection."
—Colleen Ferguson, SevenPonds.com

"Elder abuse is a growing problem—especially elder FINANCIAL abuse, which often comes at the hands of an adult child. This is worth reading."
—Terry Savage, TerrySavage.com

"This [book] is not a pleasant subject, quite frankly, but it's a very necessary subject. You can talk about the unpleasant subject and you can prepare to deal with the unpleasant subject, or you can just put on a blindfold and snowshoes and stomp into that minefield. The second course is not recommended. Prudence dictates that we do what we can to avoid this unfortunate situation."

—Jim Bohannon, Westwood One

Alzheimer's, Widowed Stepmothers & Estate Crimes

CAUSE, ACTION, AND RESPONSE IN CASES
OF FRACTURED INHERITANCE, LOST
INHERITANCE, AND DISINHERITANCE

Michael Hackard, Esq.

Hackard
Global Media

Book layout © 2018 BookDesignTemplates.com
Cover design by Olivier Darbonville

Publisher's Cataloging-In-Publication Data
(Prepared by The Donohue Group, Inc.)

Names: Hackard, Michael, Esq.
Title: Alzheimer's, widowed stepmothers & estate crimes : cause, action, and
    response in cases of fractured inheritance, lost inheritance, and disinheritance /
    Michael Hackard, Esq.
Other titles: Alzheimer's, widowed stepmothers and estate crimes
Description: Mather, CA : Hackard Global Media, [2019] | Includes bibliographical
    references and index.
Identifiers: ISBN 9780999144626 | ISBN 9780999144633 (ebook)
Subjects: LCSH: Inheritance and succession--Case studies. | Heirs--Crimes against--
    Case studies. | Older people--Finance, Personal--Case studies. | Alzheimer's
    disease--Patients--Finance, Personal--Case studies.
Classification: LCC HB715 .H33 2019 (print) | LCC HB715 (ebook) | DDC 346.05
    /2--dc23

Library of Congress Control Number: 2018914356

Hackard Global Media, LLC
10630 Mather Blvd.
Mather, CA 95655-4125

Printed in the United States of America

To my children and grandchildren, the joy of our lives.

"Every time an old person dies, it's like
a library burning down."

—ALEX HALEY

Contents

Preface i

Introduction 1

Mental Capacity and Lost Inheritance 6

Disinheritance and Cognitive Decline 18

Dad Had Alzheimer's, So I Have a Good Case, Right? 29

Why Aren't Estates Bulletproof? 40

The Widowed Stepmother 54

Problem Trustee Removal 65

Unequal Inheritance: Siblings and Half-Siblings 75

No Will, No Way? Not Necessarily 86

Safes and Safe Deposit Boxes 100

Fraud and Fraud Detection 108

Cons and Caretakers 119

Acknowledgments 129

Notes 133

Index 143

PREFACE

In the fall of 2017, I published my first book, *The Wolf at the Door: Undue Influence and Elder Financial Abuse*. I focused on a troubling issue that I have regularly confronted in my many years of legal practice. My hope was that anyone suffering from elder financial abuse, or anyone with a loved one who was suffering, would find strategies in the book to help them stop the cycle and act against the perpetrator(s) causing them harm.

The book seems to have resonated with many people. More than two dozen outlets either interviewed me about the book or ran an excerpt from it, including well-known national publications such as *MarketWatch*, *TheStreet*, *Fox Business*, and *MSN Money*. This told me that there was a dearth of good information out there on the legal challenges that can come with aging.

So, why this second book? I've come to believe more needs to be said about the challenges our seniors (and their families) face beyond elder financial abuse. Sadly, elder financial abuse is just one of the many difficulties American seniors are likely to be confronted with. By casting a bright light on Alzheimer's and dementia and their potentially devastating consequences on trusts, estates, inheritances, and family legacies, I hope to arm readers with even more practical knowledge.

Baby boomers like me, once celebrated for our youth and vigor, now face an inevitable decline brought on by aging. Our numbers—some 75 million—demand more awareness when it comes to protecting elders from those who would do them harm, especially when it comes to Alzheimer's and other forms of cognitive decline.

The scourge of Alzheimer's frightens our generation. While the disease is now better understood than it has been, it is no more curable today than it was fifty years ago. With 5.5 million Americans predicted to be suffering from the disease, it is both ubiquitous and substantially undiagnosed. One in ten Americans age sixty-five and older has Alzheimer's or a related form of dementia. Even more alarmingly, a recent study indicated that more than fifty percent of doctors neglected to inform elders with Alzheimer's or their caregivers that the elder had the disease.[1] This failure to diagnose puts victims at greater risk. The danger level only rises further when society neglects to implement necessary protections for elders with decreased cognitive and physical abilities.

Estate crimes grow from the vulnerability of our elders and a failure to shield them from abuse. Protecting America's elders is not easy, though. Our lawmakers, federal and state, are working on new measures to provide further protections. But such safeguards, however new or creative, are not effective unless families, neighbors, communities, and law enforcement share in the duty, whether through legal or community-based means, to protect our elders and secure their inheritance wishes.

The recognition that blended families may bring particular complexities to the inheritance process is another topic I explore in this book. This fact, upon reflection, is neither surprising nor unexpected. Inheritance is an idea based on expectations—expectations that we will inherit or receive the estates of our parents. The shattering of these expectations brings repercussions, whether emotional or financial. The high prevalence of second marriages in the United States, coupled with the (large) spread between female and male longevity, makes surviving stepmothers the common focus of estate disputes when they involve blended families.

An unstated backdrop to the issues of Alzheimer's, blended families, and estate crimes is that we regularly struggle with providing the proper treatment for our elders. How many of us have seen and felt the sadness of an elder who is moved from their own home into a hospital, nursing facility, or elder care home? Such removals at times seem like the only option when mom or dad can't care for themselves and are in continual danger from falling or the avarice of abusers. But they still make us question if we did the "right" thing.

Nevertheless, there are bright spots and reasons to be hopeful. Almost one in five Americans lives in a multigenerational household. Such an arrangement, which is becoming increasingly common, provides some antidote to the loneliness of elders endemic to removal from their homes into institutional settings. Elders, even in their last illnesses, are often returning to, or staying in, their own homes—the places where they lived, shared their love, and made their memories.

Our Judeo-Christian heritage teaches us to honor our fathers and our mothers, and I believe most people sincerely want to do what is right. When our parents' physical and mental abilities are waning, many families strive to venerate and guard them. If parts of our world treat our elders as castaways, others serve as a strong counterbalance. Greek culture honors old age and identifies it with wisdom and closeness to God. Young Koreans are taught that they must care for older members of the family, and each family member's seventieth birthday is a celebration of the "old and rare." Similar honor and respect are shown throughout many cultures and serve as encouraging examples.

Based on the many comments I received about *The Wolf at the Door*, I am now acutely aware of the privilege that an author is granted by readers, and I remain obliged to honor and respect that relationship. As you read what I have written, you are inviting me into your home. I will be your guest, and I hope that I will be both courteous and respectful of you and your family. I am grateful for the opportunity to share my knowledge with you and hope that our collective respect and protection of America's elders will make a difference in the lives of many.

Michael Hackard
Mather, California
October 2018

INTRODUCTION

Inheritance is an idea with rich financial, emotional, social, and spiritual connotations, but we tend to forget that today, in the modern world, it is a completely artificial legal construct. Ten thousand years ago, when someone died, what became of that person's belongings? No one can say for sure, but more than likely whatever decisions were made were pragmatic and obvious.

Since laws were created, however, things have gotten much more complicated. Common sense may once have dictated that a useful blade should be passed down to the best hunter in a group, but what about a collection of knives owned by a craftsman who had twelve children? And what about the debts that man owed? And what about his other worldly possessions?

To resolve increasingly complex sets of circumstances, civilizations created ever more elaborate sets of inheritance laws. But along that historical path, something else remarkable happened: inheritance itself began to take on new meaning. No longer just a simple process regulating the distribution of physical objects, inheritance started shaping family lore and history. Considerations of fairness—and unfairness—became integral concepts, as tangible and important as the property or objects themselves.

This is true in my own family, which was once made up of farmers. Several generations ago, one brother inherited what was considered more fertile land, while another brother got the perceived lesser tract. Generations of family members subsequently identified themselves as much by that single decision handed down from a dying man as by anything else that happened in their lives. What someone gets—or doesn't get—can reverberate through the ages, and in my family, it still does.

All of which is to say, inheritance has come to take on a far greater importance beyond just objects and property. It is about perpetuating a lineage, loyalty and faith, protection and provision, and often about the perpetuation of the memory of the dead. Fulfilling this multifaceted mission has become the goal of both law and tradition.

In American history, inheritance has been a complicated affair. America's early settlers hoped to break with an order that bestowed power and opportunity through wealth transfers based on patriarchy and biology and tried to replace it with an economic system that rewarded work and virtue over ancestral privilege. Later immigrants, however, often encountered painful prejudice in their new home country, and such bias ignited a break with Old World traditions and a rejection of one's ancestry. Immigrant children were often not taught their parents' native tongue, to make their assimilation easier. Americans, collectively, seemed to want to forget their inheritance.

That attitude changed, in part, in 1977, when *Roots*, the TV miniseries based on Alex Haley's bestselling book, captured the attention and imaginations of 130 million Americans. Suddenly heritage became something to be interested in and proud of, and this new era inspired a genealogy boom and TV series like *Who Do You Think You Are?* Today, more than ever, we care about lineage. "In all of us there is a hunger, marrow-deep, to know our heritage—to know who we are and where we have come from," wrote Haley. "Without this enriching knowledge, there is a hollow yearning. No matter what our attainments in life, there is still a vacuum, an emptiness, and the most disquieting loneliness."[1]

Just as we have begun to care deeply about where we came from, we have also come to care about how our heritage was cut off. Indeed, some people have been so disturbed by the events and actions of previous generations that they have gone to extraordinary lengths to right perceived wrongs and reclaim what they believe was an inheritance unjustly taken away. In one sensational case from 1976, a fourteen-year-old boy from Boston named William Lobkowicz visited his ancestral home in Czechoslovakia for the first time. There he learned that his ancestors had been noblemen and patrons of the arts for centuries until the family was stripped of its possessions when a Communist regime took over Czechoslovakia in 1948. In 1989, when the Communist government fell, Lobkowicz decided to move back, and he legally reclaimed his ancestral home. Today, Prince William, as he is now known, maintains four of the ten castles and palaces once owned by the House of Lobkowicz. Who would have ever thought it was possible to reclaim an ancestral home seized forty years earlier?

Unfortunately, happy stories of inheritances rightfully recovered are extremely rare—much more common are stories filled with trauma and remorse. This is especially true when it comes to families with members suffering from Alzheimer's disease or dementia. Five hundred thousand new cases of Alzheimer's and dementia are diagnosed each year in the United States, and nearly 6 million Americans are currently afflicted. In every case, the potential for inheritance problems is significantly increased.

Part of this is because blended families have become the new normal in America; according to the Stepfamily Foundation, more than 50 percent of US families now include parents who are remarried or recoupled. Blended families are significantly more likely to suffer from conflict, and, as a consequence, disinheritances, lost inheritances, and fractured inheritances now occur with shocking regularity. When such things happen, it results in a brutal break from the past—a break that shames, wounds, and lingers through generations.

This is a book about the root causes of inheritance problems, as well as the main factors that lead to inheritance plans being thwarted. These situations usually result in dashed expectations—expectations that family members will be protected, provided for, and aided in their time of need. The book offers real-life family stories, including chronicles of generations split apart, narratives of exodus—of flight, of dispossession, of success and failure—and tales of hushed but lingering wrongs. Some may be challenging to absorb, but these stories are told with a purpose: to help the millions of Americans poised to suffer from inheritance complications minimize their emotional and financial distress.

As an estate and trust attorney who has practiced law for more than forty years, I have witnessed countless family battles over inheritances: stepmothers fighting stepchildren, brothers fighting sisters, cousins fighting cousins, and more. I have witnessed the cognitive abilities of lifelong friends decline precipitously, leading them to become victims of elder financial abuse. And I have heard countless tales from clients and prospective clients whose family assets were plundered by brazen criminals who believed they could get away with it just because they thought no one was watching.

Through all those experiences, I have also learned that there are useful lessons we can draw from taking a hard look at the main three causes of inheritances gone awry: Alzheimer's, widowed stepmothers, and estate crimes. Accordingly, this book is divided into three parts, each covering one of these causes. Each part is related to the others in many ways, but also focuses in depth on the unique cause it explores. For those engaged in inheritance struggles, this book may help you figure out how to gain some measure of justice. And for those who wish to have all the facts before their upcoming inheritance, this book offers a helpful primer on things to avoid or watch out for.

It is my sincere hope that this book will be not just informative but deeply useful to those who may be on the cusp of disinheritance, a lost inheritance, or unequal inheritance. When it comes to inheritance, more is at stake than just objects and property, though they may be important. What matters ultimately are the family histories that can so easily be fractured through disputes, disease, and crimes, but which may not be completely irreparable.

Mental Capacity and Lost Inheritance

The will is on file in the local probate court. It's black and white and clear as day. An attorney drafted the documents, and a notary public witnessed them, which means that the game is over—you lost. Time to move on, right? Can you fight such an uphill battle? More to the point, is it even worth it for you to fight?

Every week I get twenty to twenty-five new e-mails and phone calls from across California asking me to hear the details of a lost inheritance or disinheritance case. The stories are heartbreaking. Grandma Marge had dementia, and her caregiver persuaded her to change her will and trust. Grandpa Joe's Parkinson's was so bad that he couldn't talk and couldn't hold a pen, but there is a copy of a new will, with a barely intelligible signature, that cuts out all his children except the substance-abusing son living with him.

When a loved one loses the capacity to make decisions, bad things can and do happen, usually to the advantage of one person and the detriment of others. The two factors frequently go hand in hand.

If you were to call me about a possible case of lost inheritance or disinheritance involving mental incapacity, I would tell you this: Before you decide to fight for a lost inheritance, you first have to understand a little bit about the practice of law and our legal system. I will offer some extreme examples to prove this point.

If someone walks into a bank with a toy gun and hands a note to a teller demanding $50,000, there is an extremely high probability that that person will go to jail. Attempted armed robbery, even if the perpetrator doesn't get away with it, is a serious crime, and you can be certain that the FBI and local law enforcement will use every available means to track the person down and bring them to justice. Indeed, even a first-time offender can expect a harsh sentence.

But if someone uses undue influence to persuade a cognitively impaired senior citizen to transfer $50,000 to their account, there is an extremely low probability that they will go to jail—and an even lower probability that they will ever disgorge a penny of their ill-gotten gains. There is no security camera, no witnesses, and often no clear evidence when it comes to undue influence. Who is to say whether or not the senior citizen was cognitively impaired? It's a judgment call, which is often not clear-cut. It is hard to prove 1) that the senior citizen was unduly influenced, 2) that the senior citizen was cognitively impaired, and 3) that the senior citizen wouldn't have wanted to make the transfer anyway.

Practicality

In financial matters that involve substantial sums taken from elders or diverted to wrongdoers because of undue influence or other wrongful conduct, it is almost certainly worth hiring an attorney to explore your legal options. But if that lost inheritance is not substantial, even if it includes everything in an estate, it may not be worth the time, expense, and emotional turmoil that is often required to pursue a case. This is a sad acknowledgment that even though a case is meritorious, the costs to prevail may far exceed the recovery. Unfortunately, our legal system is not designed to help victims of elder financial abuse as quickly or efficiently as it is to help society catch armed robbers. Ironically, the sums taken from heirs and beneficiaries by estate and trust wrongdoing are often much greater than the $7,500 that the FBI reports as the average sum stolen by bank robbers.

Here is how I generally handle inquiries made to my firm: We take on estate, trust, and elder financial abuse cases where we believe we can make a significant difference, and where there is a defendant or respondent who can be made financially accountable for their wrongdoing. There are times when we will pursue a wrongdoer who has committed a grave injustice even though we know the ultimate remedy may provide little economic return to our law firm. This is not to say that I am the lawyer of last resort; the economics of a law practice still enter into the equation. That said, we do our share of pro bono work on cases that cry out for justice.

Where do I, or any other lawyer for that matter, draw the general economic lines? Each firm makes this decision differently, but this is the pragmatic template I typically use:

1) Is the case large enough for us to justify representation? Unlike many other firms, mine works almost exclusively on contingency fees, which

means that we often absorb enormous costs upfront.

2) Under California law, does the conduct of the wrongdoer constitute elder financial abuse? If so, then we know that we have a civil case with a defendant who is not supposed to be using trust assets to defend themselves. In a civil case, there is a lower burden of proof; the legal standard is "a preponderance of the evidence," which means that if we are successful in an elder financial abuse case, the wrongdoer may be responsible for attorney's fees.

3) Lastly, and also of great importance, is the fact that in a civil case we can request a jury trial. As an experienced advocate I favor the jury trial system; our chances of persuading a group of reasonable laypeople of wrongdoing might be more promising than convincing a single battle-weary judge in probate court.

No matter who takes the case, the costs quickly escalate. A typical elder financial abuse case involving mental incapacity and lost inheritance can easily require three hundred to eight hundred attorney hours, and most attorneys who focus in this area charge $400 an hour. Someone might be surprised or offended when an attorney says that the expected return of $300,000 won't cover the attorney's fees, but that can certainly be true. If a case demands depositions and testimony from medical experts, that can add another $40,000 or more.

It may sound harsh, but you should know that I write this not to dissuade anyone from pursuing a legitimate case but rather to forewarn you what to expect. It's not always a pure dollars and cents decision, but smaller estate cases will more typically be taken on by younger attorneys who need the experience more than the billable hours.

The good news is that if someone does have a case of lost inheritance or disinheritance involving diminished mental capacity or cognitive decline, and if the amount at stake can cover contingency fees, there is a reasonable probability of recovery and success. If a prodigal son persuaded Mom, who had Alzheimer's, to exclusively give him her $800,000 house in the foothills of Los Angeles, there is a reasonable chance that an experienced attorney can see that the rightful heirs share in the estate despite the existence of any questionable documents.

Alzheimer's Disease, Lewy Body Dementia, and Cognitive Decline

Doctors don't like to share a diagnosis of Alzheimer's disease with their patients or patients' families.[1] That's an unfortunate fact. Sometimes it's because doctors, nurses, and physician's assistants aren't trained to look for the signs. A new law in Massachusetts, the first of its kind in the United States, aims to change that by requiring special training before such professionals can obtain or renew their licenses.[2]

As we get older, we tend to forget more, and there may be a multitude of medical reasons why someone can seem confused or disoriented. CT and MRI scans can be inconclusive, which means that making a clear-cut diagnosis as to the source of some cognitive decline is hard. Add to that the fact that doctors are in the business of saving lives, and giving someone a diagnosis of Alzheimer's is tantamount to handing down a death sentence, certainly no easy task. It would not surprise me if more than 50 percent of all cases of Alzheimer's and related diseases go undiagnosed.

Here's an example of a situation we often see in my practice: A potential client contacts us to discuss his disinheritance from his mother's trust. We learn that his mother just died. He then provides us with a copy of an amendment to her trust from a few years earlier disinheriting him. We ask the son, "What was happening when the amendment was made?" We want to know about his mother's cognitive ability at the time.

These types of cases often require the services of a psychiatrist with a specialty in gerontology. They serve as experts who can take a look at a decedent's medical records and identify the potential causes of a degeneration in cognitive ability. Oftentimes the psychiatrist may not find incapacity, but only because the issue did not arise in such a way that it could be documented. There may be no smoking gun that clearly demonstrates cognitive decline. In the case of the mother mentioned above, a forensic analysis by a psychiatrist, neuropsychologist, or other expert in gerontology might be needed to establish her state of mind around the time she made the amendment to her trust. That can be, and usually is, a long, drawn-out, expensive process.

If someone disinherits a relative in the last few years of their life it does not necessarily mean that they had cognitive decline or Alzheimer's disease. But it is fair to say that if someone has Alzheimer's or is otherwise cognitively impaired, their decision-making ability is compromised. Like it or not, that's just true. Some disinherited plaintiffs may deserve to be cut off, but how can anyone know for sure? As an attorney, I work to identify reasonable causes of disinheritance or lost inheritance and represent my clients to the best of my ability. To that end, the first question I seek to answer is whether or not the decedent was cognitively impaired. Figuring this out tends to be easier when a doctor has already made a diagnosis, but a medical label alone will not prove or resolve a case.

Game Plans

I am comfortable with our civil litigation system. As a litigator with more than forty years of experience in courtrooms across America, I have had an extraordinary vista of the processes in place that facilitate compensation to injured parties by those who injured them. In fact, since my firm litigates, a new case for us always contains the possibility of a court fight. That said, these cases often end up in mediation. It surprises most of my clients to hear that in the United States 97 percent of all civil cases settle before trial.

While every new case is filed in civil or probate court, most of the time the parties and their counsel realize that a case settlement may be far more economical in time and treasure than a protracted trial and appeal. Such settlements are often accomplished in mediation. Mediation is not perfect, but the system is faster and much less expensive than a trial. Mediation is the process of risk assessment. In court, a party may lose it all or gain it all; in mediation, the parties may divide what is in an estate or trust. Proportionate division is often the main goal of mediation.

What to Expect in Mediation

The best mediators are usually retired superior court judges who have probate experience. Such mediators typically command $400–$1,000 per hour and usually charge a minimum of a half day's work. That said, a few of California's leading estate and trust mediators are private counsel with decades of experience in the field. The costs may sound like a lot, but a good mediator can cut through enormous issues in short order, which can save both sides massive sums compared to protracted litigation in court.

A mediator with experience in Alzheimer's and lost inheritance cases will often know how to best approach both sides to arrive at a compromise. Sometimes that is done by examining the strengths and weaknesses of each side in an unemotional way and giving each the opportunity to explain their side to the other. All of this has to be done delicately, because either side can walk out at any time.

The great benefit of mediation is that it typically brings cases to a conclusion in a single day. After months of preparation and mountains of paperwork, and if both sides agree to the process, a mediator has the power to resolve a disinheritance conflict on the spot. Is it a perfect system? Certainly not. I have been surprised at times by mediators who were unfamiliar with basic elder financial abuse law. By and large, however, most mediators know what they are doing and earn every penny of their fee!

Cognitive Impairment and How to Protect the Ones You Love

Let me walk you through some common scenarios involving Alzheimer's and cognitive impairment. This will, I hope, give you a sense of how most of these types of cases proceed. Every fact pattern is unique, of course, and circumstances are often extenuating, so you can't rely on this information to fit every scenario. But it will help you understand the thought process and typical steps during litigation.

We can begin with an overview of the problem. Cognitive decline in the elderly affects all areas of their lives, and that holds true for their financial accounts, estates, and trusts. Some unscrupulous predators jump at the chance to take advantage of the elderly, the confused, the lonely.[3] Most of this wrongdoing is unconscionable, but sociopathic individuals share none of our concern for another's well-being. Some of them are even family members, an unfortunate but all-too-common reality in many of the cases we litigate.

Fraud and abuse appear in many forms. Scammers use e-mail, snail mail, and the telephone to ensnare victims and commit identity theft and credit card fraud. A supposedly "friendly" neighbor might offer to mow the lawn for the friendly sum of $500 a week. And, worst of all, a family member (often a substance abuser) can isolate, threaten, or manipulate an elder and then go on to loot their estate or trust. Undue influence is more common than you might think.[4]

What can you do to spot and prevent elder financial abuse and keep an elder with Alzheimer's safe? Be a diligent investigator—ask the right questions. Here are some good ones to start with:

- Are bills left unpaid or have utilities been shut off due to non-payment?[5]

- Do checks or estate documents have unfamiliar or odd signatures that don't match the elder's?

- Has the elder's will been changed without their full comprehension or approval?

- Did someone sell the elder's home without their approval?

- Has the elder been made to sign other legal documents, like power of attorney or a joint deed to a house, without understanding what they mean?

- Have valuable items gone missing in the elder's house? Are there irregularities in their bank accounts?

Finding the answers to these questions will bring you closer to stopping any wrongdoing that may be underway. If you encounter evidence of theft, your first call should be to local law enforcement.

Practical Steps When You've Been Cut Out of a Will or Trust

What are your options if you are cut out of a family will or trust? Whether the will or trust in question is in Sacramento, San Mateo, or Los Angeles, exploring your options is a critical part of decision-making. In probate, estate, and trust litigation the "ready, shoot, aim" approach is not particularly effective. With this in mind here are five things to remember.

1) Calculate Estimated Damages

Whether you are involved in a case of disinheritance, contested wills, delayed and denied distributions, executor wrongdoing, trustee misconduct, or dozens of other estate-related incidents that regularly arise, you have to make a cold and hard calculation: "How much is at stake?"

Remember that grief, anger, and a sense of betrayal can accompany an estate dispute, and this can blind wronged parties to a realistic assessment of the damages. Painful though it may be, sometimes the smartest decision is to walk away. When in doubt, consult an experienced attorney.

2) Remember that Time Is of the Essence

Settlements usually happen after a lawsuit is filed, not before. That said, experienced counsel on opposite sides of a dispute might explore settlement early, as they know the costs and burdens of litigation.

The law does not reward those who delay seeking their rights. There are often very restrictive time limits for filing will and trust litigation matters. In California, trust challenges must be filed within a 120-day window after a trust beneficiary receives notice that a trust is irrevocable, for example, and courts do not grant extensions.

3) Do Your Homework

I always ask clients to help me prepare a timeline of the facts in the case. We also need to know what the current status of the case is. Did the executor, the person appointed by the court to handle the estate, sell the estate's assets and move to Ecuador? Or is he still in town and enjoying his new Cadillac? Is there a probate pending or trust administration case pending in a Probate Court?

4) Make a Plan

Remember the adage "He who fails to plan, plans to fail." Hire an experienced California estate litigation lawyer to assist you. Remember that an internet search does not make you an expert. The probate litigator probably knows quite a lot more than you could know through a four-hour Google search.

Identify the steps in your plan. Figure out how the costs of estate litigation will be paid. Hourly? On contingency? A combination of a reduced hourly rate with a contingency fee?

5) Figure Out If You Want a Jury Trial

There are special rules governing the availability of jury trials in probate and estate matters. My firm files matters in both the civil and probate divisions of the California Superior Court system. Matters filed in the civil division often have a statutory right to a jury trial—an important right, to be sure. There are some matters that by law belong and stay in the probate division of the superior court. In probate court a judge makes the final ruling, which is sometimes an advantage and at other times a disadvantage. The calculus of whether to file in probate or civil court depends on the law and whether a jury trial is desired.

Disinheritance and Cognitive Decline

Tony Curtis was a Hollywood icon, an actor who appeared in more than one hundred films, a World War II veteran who served honorably in the navy aboard a submarine, and an actor who was nominated for two Golden Globes, an Emmy, and an Oscar. He was a major star who acted alongside Frank Sinatra, Cary Grant, Jack Lemmon, and Kirk Douglas. He also starred with Marilyn Monroe in the hit 1959 comedy *Some Like It Hot*.

Despite his enormous success, his death was hastened by years of cigarette smoking, alcoholism, and cocaine addiction. When Curtis died in 2010 at the age of eighty-five, he left behind a rich film legacy, six wives, five children, and seven grandchildren. In a surprise to them, however, he left behind only one heir, who inherited his $40 million estate—his sixth wife, Jill Vandenberg Curtis, forty-five years his junior.[1] All of his children were disinherited.

To make matters worse, a year after Curtis died, his widow sold hundreds of personal effects and memorabilia at an auction that netted more than $1 million.[2] None of his children, including the actresses Jamie Lee Curtis and Allegra Curtis, received any of the proceeds. Why? Because a year before he died, Curtis wrote a new will and redid his trust, which effectively disinherited all his children.[3]

The Curtis case, like many other celebrity elder financial abuse cases, springs from a less-than-amicable relationship between a widowed stepmother and her stepchildren. Of course, it likely didn't help that Curtis's widow was considerably younger than all her stepchildren.[4]

For someone in his mid-eighties and not in good health to suddenly change his will and trust to disinherit children is a red flag and deeply suspicious. In my legal experience, such late changes to an estate, especially ones involving stepmothers and stepchildren, nearly always lead to litigation. When Curtis's shocked children received the news, their initial reaction was predictable. There were public charges of "duress, menace, fraud and undue influence."[5]

From multiple press reports in the months following his death, we also learned that the relationship between Curtis and his children was strained. Perhaps they didn't get along. Perhaps he felt that they were all financially self-sufficient and therefore did not need to inherit any of his wealth.

Or perhaps, as his children alleged, he was not mentally capable of understanding the implications of his actions.[6] Perhaps someone else did his thinking for him.

The prose from his will, however, was clear enough. He wrote: "I acknowledge the existence of my children

. . . and have intentionally and with full knowledge chosen not to provide for them in this last will and testament."[7]

In the end, Curtis's children quickly dropped the suit against their stepmother and brought the matter to a close. Since most of them were actors and public figures, perhaps they believed that continuing with a lawsuit would cause reputational damage. Maybe they did not, after all, need the money. Proving that mental impairment was the reason their father had disinherited his children would have been expensive and difficult, though certainly not impossible.

Disinheritance is a complicated and complex subject. As an attorney, I have found that resolving disinheritance issues is always messy, often protracted, never simple, and not always successful. The truth is that if you've been disinherited, for whatever reason, the chances of your getting a "full" share of an estate are usually low. Here are some of the obvious and frequent reasons why people are disinherited:

- Their parent(s) didn't like them.

- They lost touch with their parent and didn't contact them for ten years (and sometimes much longer).

- Their parent had a favorite child and gave everything to them.

- Their sibling(s) poisoned the waters and said horrible things about them (perhaps truthfully, perhaps falsely), which caused the parent to disinherit.

- They squandered a fortune earlier in life, and their parent made a rational decision not to throw good estate money after bad.

If disinheritance is a result of one of the above factors, it is unlikely (though, again, not impossible) that an attorney can do much. Inheritance laws allow people to choose very precisely who gets what from their estate. If Grandpa wants to cut a prodigal child from his inheritance, he has every right to do so.

As a practical matter, however, there are always extenuating circumstances, and human relationships are never black and white. Maybe a sibling or some other caregiver exerted undue influence over the elder during a period of vulnerability. Maybe Grandpa had a degenerative brain disease and wasn't thinking clearly at the moment when he signed his will. Maybe Grandpa didn't realize that he had disinherited someone in a will he wrote twenty years ago when they weren't on good terms, and simply neglected to update his will once the relationship improved. There is an infinite number of reasons why someone might contest disinheritance, and therefore an infinite number of ways that an attorney can approach the problem.

All that said, in many cases where someone has been disinherited, he or she has received nothing because they deserved nothing. Grandpa had good reasons for writing them out of his will. Keep in mind that neither the law nor life is ever black and white.

Another Word About Attorney's Fees

Sometimes disinherited people call me, and I'm forced to make a snap judgment about whether their case merits my digging deeper. Were they unintentionally wronged? Was there an injustice done to them? Were they the abused or the abuser? Of course, it's not up to me or any other attorney to pass moral judgment about prospective clients, and there is no way I can ever know what actually transpired in any family situation, but I would rather not work hard on behalf of someone unless I truly believe that an injustice has occurred. Someone could have certainly been a bad son or daughter, but that doesn't necessarily mean that the ones who wound up with the inheritance were any better. So, while I don't decide to take on a case based on whether or not I like someone personally, I won't take a case unless I firmly believe that a prospective client was wronged.

For those who seek action, there may be difficulties in paying for an estate and trust litigation attorney. As noted in Chapter 1, litigating estate claims is always expensive, so such cases typically, though not always, involve estates that exceed $1 million. If someone successfully contests a disinheritance claim involving a $100,000 estate, but the associated fees (court fees, attorney's fees, investigation fees, professional fees) are likely to exceed $200,000, there may be a pyrrhic victory at stake, and certainly not a case any thoughtful attorney would ever want to take. Where the stakes are bigger, and there is an injustice that needs addressing, hourly fees, contingency fees, or a combination of reduced hourly rates and reduced contingency fees are payment options that can be explored and negotiated between an attorney and client.

Representation based on contingency fees may be available when a money recovery or something of considerable value such as real estate can be awarded. (Remember that in these cases attorney's fees are based entirely on a favorable outcome.) Such agreements generally specify that the contingency fee percentage will apply to any award, verdict, judgment, settlement, or compromise.[8]

If the recovery consists of payments made over a period of time, arrangements can be made that calculate the present cash value of the stream of income, with the attorney's fees paid out of the first funds or property received by the client.

Contingency fee agreements may be your key to having a fighting chance in the courtroom. Not all cases are appropriate for contingency fees, and the arrangement is ultimately dependent on a willing attorney and a willing client. In any such situation, written fee agreements with proper disclosures are required.[9]

To Fight or Not to Fight?

Before contesting disinheritance, there are a few important questions beyond the simple economic one: namely, is the case worth it? Here are a few questions you need to answer before you can decide if it's time to fight or fold:

- **Is there a valid will?** A valid will is one that meets all the legal and statutory requirements of the law and was signed by the deceased at a point when they were "of sound mind." How can you ever tell what the mental state of an individual is? There are no easy answers, and this question is often answered in court by deposing witnesses and getting expert testimony. The burden of proof is often steep, and the costs to prove the validity of a will can be enormous.

- **Was the deceased subject to undue influence?** The subject of undue influence could fill an entire book, and indeed, my first book, *The Wolf at the Door: Undue Influence and Elder Financial Abuse*, covers this subject extensively. Undue influence can be exerted in both subtle and obvious ways, and how such cases go depends largely on the facts of each case. Proving undue influence is a process, but there is a clear path to victory if there are sufficient facts to support the charge.

- **Is the language of the will fuzzy?** Sometimes what seems clear-cut isn't. A person's will may state that they choose not to give someone an inheritance because they believe that they have "sufficient resources" or are "otherwise provided for." What does that mean? Maybe your idea of "sufficient" isn't the same as my idea. Who wins that argument? Often a court needs to decide.

Accidental Disinheritance and Cognitive Decline

Suppose you were simply not mentioned in the will at all. Suppose Grandpa wrote his will before you were born and never bothered to update it once you became an important part of his life. Does that mean you are just out of luck? Fortunately, in cases of accidental disinheritance, there is quite a lot that can be done to rectify the situation. Let's assume that the maker of the will, the testator (also referred to as the decedent), has died and you discover that you are not mentioned in their will. Here are some initial points of inquiry.

- What is your familial relationship with the decedent?

- Are you a spouse?

- Are you a child of the decedent?

- Are you a child of the predeceased spouse of a decedent?

- Are you a child of a predeceased child of a decedent (a grandchild)?

- Are you a sibling?

Your rights will be determined in part by your familial relationship. For example, spousal rights depend on the nature of the ownership of the decedent's real and personal property. In California, an asset acquired or income earned while living with a spouse is considered "community property"; each spouse owns one half of it. Upon the death of a spouse, one half of the community property belongs to the surviving spouse, and the other half belongs to the decedent. The decedent only has power of disposition over their half of community property—not the surviving spouse's half. This issue sometimes arises when the maker of a will tries to bequeath both halves of community property (like a house) to someone other than the surviving spouse. It doesn't work, but the mix-up may put the surviving spouse into an estate fight with someone who doesn't know the law. The community property of a decedent who dies without a will (an intestate) automatically passes to their surviving spouse.

"Separate property" is defined as anything acquired by each spouse before their marriage or during the marriage by gift, devise, or bequest, and property acquired after the parties separate. The decedent has full power of the disposition over their separate property. All of an intestate's separate property passes to their spouse if they don't have any surviving children. If there are surviving children, the surviving spouse receives one third (if there are two or more children) to one half (if there is only one child) of the deceased spouse's separate property.

In California and most other states, if a deceased spouse's will was executed before the marriage and fails to provide for their surviving spouse, the survivor is entitled to a share of the deceased spouse's estate. This share includes a one-half share of any community property and one third (if there are two or more children) to one half (if there is only one child) of the deceased spouse's separate property.

A child of a predeceased spouse of a decedent may have rights to their stepparent's intestate estate. (A predeceased spouse is a person who died before the decedent while married to the decedent.) In California, there is a law that allows children of a predeceased spouse to inherit property of an intestate stepparent provided that certain conditions are met. This law allows the stepchildren to inherit a deceased stepparent's property if 1) the property was inherited from the stepchildren's natural parent and 2) the stepparent dies without a surviving spouse or issue. "Issue" refers to a person's lineal descendants of all generations (children, grandchildren, etc.).

In the Case of Blended Families

Why are inheritance-related questions so likely to arise in blended families? For one, given the high incidence of divorce in the United States, at least half of America's children live with a biological parent and a stepparent. Blended families face many unique challenges, among them different parenting styles, conflicting emotions, and the natural stresses associated with changes in home life. Sibling rivalry may spring up between biological children and stepsiblings. In many families, there are invisible psychological bonds that favor biological children over stepchildren.

Simple facts of life also play a part. Longevity for Americans over the age of fifty is expected to exceed that of previous generations. Statistically speaking, women are likely to live significantly longer than men, and this gap has widened over the years; today, it is close to seven years in the United States. So it stands to reason that there will be more widowed stepmothers than widowed stepfathers. In fact, in the United States, it is estimated that there are 11.2 million widowed stepmothers and 2.9 million widowed stepfathers.

When a biological parent is in cognitive decline, they are susceptible to undue influence. Undue influence is excessive persuasion that causes another person to act, or refrain from acting, by overcoming that person's free will, and it results in inequity. Here's a relatively common example, and one that often triggers estate, trust, or elder financial abuse litigation: A father, vulnerable to others because of Alzheimer's, incapacity, illness, or some other factor, is coerced to change his estate plan to give virtually everything to his second or third spouse. The father's previous estate plan provided for an equal division between his biological children and his surviving spouse; the later estate plan, however, completely excludes his biological children. When his surviving children learn of the changes after his death, they naturally feel abandoned and betrayed. These emotions are potent kindling for estate fights.

Absent cognitive decline, estate plans allocating an inheritance to both biological children and a surviving spouse often remain unchanged, because grounds for mounting a challenge are harder to prove in such cases, and everyone received *something*, which means fewer people have a reason to challenge the estate. It is the change that triggers the estate and trust fights, fights that can be quite destructive to estate assets and ultimate inheritances. In either case, whether the estate plan was changed or not, when a father disinherits his biological children there are ways for surviving children to address the issue. Intentional or unintentional disinheritance happens routinely, but an experienced attorney has ways to fight for the heirs. Tony Curtis's children may not have needed the money they would have gotten from an inheritance, but most others won't be that lucky. For them, there may be good legal options.

Dad Had Alzheimer's, So I Have a Good Case, Right?

The name John Seward Johnson I probably means very little to you, but you certainly know the company that Johnson's father, Robert Wood Johnson, cofounded. Johnson & Johnson, the maker of baby products we've all used for generations, is a multibillion-dollar corporation that produces an array of healthcare products.

By the time Robert Wood Johnson died of cancer in 1983, at the age of eighty-seven, he left an estate of more than $400 million, equivalent to more than $1 billion in 2018 dollars. Unfortunately for his heirs, he also left behind a complicated estate battle that took years and millions of dollars to sort out. His six children, from his first two marriages, alleged that Johnson was not mentally competent when he left his fortune to his third wife, Barbara Piasecka Johnson, a chambermaid forty-two years his junior whom he married in 1971. The fact that none of his children attended the wedding is a good indication of how they felt about the union.

Johnson's contested will stemmed from a decision he made in the last year of his life. He changed his will at the age of eighty-seven, leaving everything to Piasecka. His family members, all extremely wealthy and with the means to wage legal war, immediately retained the services of the top law firms in New York City.

When millions of dollars are on the line, the stakes are high, and families pull out all the stops to get what they believe is warranted. In the Johnson case—or I should say, cases; ultimately there were at least three separate lawsuits filed—the family member litigants spent millions to produce witnesses willing to corroborate their version of the facts. In one case, a former longtime employee of John Seward Johnson was paid $160,000 ostensibly for "caretaker work"; in actuality, it was a way to get him to testify as a witness.[1]

In addition to the multiple lawsuits the heirs brought, the cases also produced legal complaints against their lawyers. One lawyer for Piasecka, for example, was brought before the Disciplinary Committee of the Appellate Division of the State Supreme Court in New York for allegedly bribing witnesses to testify on her behalf. According to the complaint, the attorney "perpetrated this scheme by paying extraordinary sums of money to some witnesses who became beholden to them and by threatening and intimidating others who did not."[2]

In the end, everyone made out well. The executor of the estate earned $8 million in fees, plus an annual trustee fee of $900,000. The attorneys on all sides earned millions in fees. And Barbara Piasecka Johnson agreed to pay out $200 million, which was divided among the children and ex-wives, leaving the J & J widow with a fortune of $300 million that grew to more than $2 billion by the time she died in 2013. In the decades that followed she became a celebrated philanthropist, so maybe her late husband chose wisely in leaving his estate to her.

The central question in all the cases was whether Robert Wood Johnson was mentally impaired when he changed his will and left everything to his third wife. That is still a good question—and one that remains unresolved. After more than four years of litigation, the cases were settled out of court, which means that no judge or jury ever ruled on the mental competency issue.

Litigation Strategies in Real Life

As extreme as the Johnson case is, it is not so different from the many cases I routinely come across in my legal practice. When an elderly person changes a will late in life with the result that some family members become disinherited or receive less of an inheritance than they expected, the issue of mental capacity is always the first question that needs to be addressed. Even with documented medical evidence, such matters are hardly ever black and white.

The public policies supporting enhanced protections for California's elderly are creating a new playbook—not one tied to traditional defense tactics (such as delays) but one that allows a jury to focus on the vulnerability of elders and damages against wrongdoers who commit bad acts. It's that simple.[3]

Simple isn't necessarily easy, however.

Even if you think you have a "good" case, does that mean that you should dive in? Dad had Alzheimer's, and you got a raw deal, so that should be simple to resolve, right? In the end, issues involving fractured inheritance need to be considered in the hard light of risks versus rewards. If you are not financially, emotionally, or even physically prepared to take on the challenge, are there alternatives to litigation?

There are. Entreaties to the better nature of an estate actor sometimes work. For example, a daughter who unduly influenced her mother to transfer the family home to her alone may upon reflection see that the action was unfair to her siblings and work to equalize the gift. A stepparent might work to settle her deceased spouse's estate by including the decedent's biological children in an estate distribution. These things do happen. But when they don't happen, the excluded heirs and trust beneficiaries may seek counsel.

Every case is different, but let me walk you through a typical scenario that results in litigation.

Litigation scenarios usually involve disinherited children in a will or excluded or abused beneficiaries in a trust. These are the people who reach out to my firm. Many of these cases also involve elder financial abuse—the taking of an elder's property through improper conduct. So let's assume that we've accepted the case. Filing deadlines may loom because of statutes of limitation or other time constraints. In California, we have only a limited window after someone dies in which to challenge a trust, for example. We gather the facts as best we can, prepare pleadings, and file them in the appropriate courts.

What we may know before filing a lawsuit will often change through a process called discovery. Discovery is the formal exchange of evidentiary information and materials (evidence) between the parties to litigation. Before the trial begins, each party is entitled to know what evidence the other party may present, unless statutory or public policy considerations clearly prohibit it. In California, discovery rules are designed to make discovery a "simple, convenient and inexpensive" means of revealing the truth.

Discovery is also designed to "educate the parties concerning their claims and defenses so as to encourage settlements and to expedite and facilitate trial."[4]

When we launch a probate litigation action in California, respondents or defendants are duly served with court papers. Discovery may progress, and there may be a number of communications between the opposing lawyers. At some point it is normal to receive a message from the opposing lawyer setting forth their perspective—call it the opening salvo. Many but not all of the letters are similar in thematic approach and the direness of their warnings.

When these letters are shared with my clients they may cause a visceral response—a response that is in part the defense's objective. Given my firm's regular litigation in the subject area, we're accustomed to these polemics. Below I've listed a few actual letters I've gotten from attorneys and my responses (in italics). These letters are what I might call "defense-speak." As a plaintiff's lawyer, I'm inclined to think that many defense lawyers work hard to skillfully deflect any facts that point to wrongdoing.

- "Nothing can be wrong with this trust because the estate-planning attorney indicates that Decedent had capacity at the time he executed the Trust." *Now that's a big surprise—an estate-planning attorney, who is supposed to at least make reasonable inquiries about capacity, says that his client had capacity.*

- "The estate-planning attorney says that there is no doubt that the defendant did not unduly influence the Decedent."[5] *This is always an interesting opinion— just what did the estate-planning lawyer do to ascertain whether their client was vulnerable to undue influence?*

- "The estate-planning attorney's testimony along with neighbors, family, and friends will prove that Decedent had capacity and he was not subject to undue influence." *This is the job of the defense lawyer: to present a credible defense. Our job is to present a credible challenge.*

- "The lawsuit for elder financial abuse is a nuisance suit designed to force the trustee to pay for his own counsel because the suit itself has absolutely no merit." *These comments are often made by probate lawyers who are unfamiliar with elder financial abuse law.*

- "Hackard Law's client has absolutely no proof of the allegations she made against her brother. In fact, Defendant's brother is considering taking action against his sister for filing such defamatory actions against him under penalty of perjury." *This is a little bit unhinged—evidence is developed over the course of discovery. Moreover, the defense lawyer is usually not aware of the evidence that we've already gathered.*

- The Hackard Law pleading is "woefully inadequate on its face, the 'evidence' on which it purports to rely does not exist." *This must go with the belief that we have no case whatsoever. If we've taken the case, we have a different opinion based on the evidence available to us before more extensive discovery.*

- The pleading has "no merit" and is "inadequate." The evidence is "conclusive" and "overwhelming" not only that the trust is valid but also that there was never elder abuse of any kind. *See above comments.*

- The defendant "had an extremely close and loving relationship" and he only took care of his mother "out of the goodness of his heart." *That must be why he froze his sisters out of communicating with his mother and why he took his mother's million-dollar estate.*

- Hackard Law's client has "violated the no-contest clause," and the client lacks probable cause to file the pleading. *We fight this one regularly, and still some lawyers keep trying.*

- Hackard Law's client "will, therefore, take nothing under the Trust, nor will any other designated beneficiary, including any contingent beneficiary, that acted with her either directly or indirectly." *Wow, you mean to say that your client is going to keep everything? We understand that this is certainly the defendant's intent—that's why there's a dispute.*

When it comes to the settlement, defense-speak is no less common:

- This is a "one-time settlement offer in an effort to conclude this matter before time and money is wasted on your client's frivolous and unsubstantiated claims." *More polemics. Cases are settled because the deal option is better than the no-deal option.*

- If Hackard Law's client doesn't accept this offer, "my client will pursue all remedies against your client including enforcement of the no-contest clause and the pursuit of a malicious prosecution claim for filing the trust contest without reasonable cause." *You mean to say that your client is upset that he might lose some of the estate that he wrongfully took? This is a defense lawyer trying to overplay his hand.*

- Hackard Law's pleadings "merely contain recycled generic allegations without any substance of supporting facts." *We don't take cases unless we think that there are supporting facts.*

- The defense lawyer's client is "outraged at the accusations" made by her brother. *Her client might very well be outraged at the accusations. She probably won't like the substantial evidence that will support the accusations, either.*

The defense's playbook is predictable: the decedent had capacity; everything that the plaintiff alleges has no merit; you better watch out—a no-contest clause and a malicious prosecution action are coming; and any abnormal changes in the estate plan are a result of the very close and loving relationship between the decedent and the alleged estate wrongdoer.

We expect the old playbook, and clients can expect that we will make every diligent effort to hold a wrongdoer accountable.[6] Conduct rewarded is conduct repeated. The bottom line is that the bluster of "defense-speak" does not work with us.

To Fight or Not to Fight? (Part 2)

Let's take a step back and see how our intake on these types of cases is done. By the time that we meet our potential new client, they should have heard that Hackard Law takes cases where 1) we believe that we can make a significant difference and 2) there is a responsible party who can be made financially accountable for their wrongdoing.

Whenever anyone calls our office, we always ask them to tell us their story. What is their particular concern? How have they identified wrongdoing in an elder financial abuse, trust, or estate matter? There is an art to the interview, and the art is honed by repetition. The essence is to identify when the wrongdoing occurred and, if possible, the timeframe during which it could have been prevented.

Basic journalist's queries apply in every estate and trust litigation interview. These are our standard questions:

- Who is the potential client?

- Who is the decedent?

- Who are other parties to the issue? The trustee? The beneficiary? The sibling(s)? The spouse?

- What is in the estate/trust? Real property? Stocks or bonds? Bank accounts?

- Where is the decedent's home? The trustee's place of business? The wrongdoer's residence?

- When did the decedent sign his or her estate plan?

- When did the decedent die?

- What is the main issue? Incapacity? Elder financial abuse? Pre-death transfers? Bank accounts? Beneficiary freeze-outs?

- Why does the potential client think that this is happening? Why does the potential client point to wrongdoing?

Once we have answers, we can apply what we know to the basics of California law when it comes to estates, trusts, and elder financial abuse. This application might be determined in a quick phone call between me and a potential client, or it might require some extensive research. If the answer seems to support a viable estate, trust, or elder financial abuse action, we will explore whether taking the case makes sense for the client and for us.

So Do I Have a Case?

Let's return to the central question posed at the beginning of this chapter: Dad had Alzheimer's, so I have a good case, right?

What I hope you realize is that every case is different, and every case has strengths and weaknesses. The fact that your dad had Alzheimer's and the fact that he cut you out of his will does not automatically mean that your case will be easy to prove. No matter what, if the dollar amounts at stake are large, opposing counsel will not simply roll over! Estate battles are messy, complicated, and often expensive, and I would not advise anyone to address an injustice unless they understand the risks and potential rewards of doing so.

Here are a few things I ask potential clients to think about before engaging the services of my firm:

- Waging an estate battle will change the way you think of the decedent, who is often a close loved one. Are you okay with that?

- Waging an estate battle will most likely irrevocably change your relationship with the other side, which in most cases is a relative. Are you prepared to sever that relationship?

- Are you doing this for the money or to gain some measure of justice?

- Will the pain of not pursuing a wrongdoer outweigh the pain of waging what may be a bruising court case?

When a decedent has Alzheimer's or some other ailment causing cognitive decline, it is very likely that a case can be made that their condition caused one or more heirs to receive less than their rightful share of inheritance. That said, costs must be balanced against potential benefits, and risks must be balanced against potential rewards. Note that someone can have a "great case" and still lose.

Here's the bottom line: Nothing in life, or in the law, is ever guaranteed, and there's no such thing as a slam-dunk estate case. Even if Dad had Alzheimer's.

4

Why Aren't Estates Bulletproof?

Prospective clients often tell me they have Googled the issues that they face, and they will share their Googled information with me, asserting that their case is "a piece of cake." Four hours of Googling may provide a good deal of information but will generate little actual knowledge. DIY research based on an internet search has helped lots of people in many areas of life, but when it comes to estate planning and trust creation, it isn't enough.

We make financial plans that are subject to market swings, global conflicts, job losses, divorces, impaired health, or other innumerable circumstances. It just comes down to this: Life is full of risks and unforeseen events. In the words of Matthew 5:45, "Your Father in heaven . . . causes his sun to rise on the bad as well as the good, and sends down rain to fall on the upright and wicked alike."

That's life. Some days are sunny, some stormy. Still, the desire for security and safety persists within each of us.

When it comes to estate planning, a settlor (the maker of a trust) or testator (the maker of a will) seeks certainty over uncertainty. They take the time to make an estate plan to diminish risks. Once this is accomplished, is the estate plan impervious to challenge? In more colloquial terms—is the will or trust bulletproof? And, if it's not bulletproof, what will it take to make it so?

My law firm's heavy estate, trust, and elder financial abuse litigation caseload precludes an active estate-planning practice. We are more often engaged in righting wrongs when someone's trust or estate plan has been breached. Our litigation frequently places a spotlight on the actions of estate lawyers before and during the preparation and execution of an estate plan. From my perspective, as an attorney who is often tasked with helping my clients by shooting holes in a will or trust document, I can report that "bulletproof" estates are a rarity, if not an impossibility.

There is little question that estate planning is helpful, but like all things it's subject to the intervention of foreseen and unforeseen events. In the words of John Lennon in "Beautiful Boy (Darling Boy)," "Life is what happens to you while you're busy making other plans."[1]

The Biggest Problem with Most Estate Plans

According to the American Association of Retired Persons (AARP), 60 percent of Americans over eighteen have no will or living trust, and even 42 percent of baby boomers (those aged fifty-three to seventy-one) have no estate-planning documents.[2] The downsides of this are obvious. Inaction allows the federal or state government to choose your "estate plan" for you, through statutes designed for intestate estates. Several factors increase the likelihood of inaction when it comes to estate planning. These include:

- Avoidance of contemplating your own death

- Lack of contact with your children

- Misunderstanding estate laws

- The belief that your estate is too small for planning

- Leaving it to the kids to "work out"

- The desire to avoid brewing differences over your estate plans between spouses

As we get older, all these issues are magnified. Why? Because the older you are when you write a will or trust document, the more likely an attorney can make the argument that you lacked capacity at the time your document was signed. There is generally a three-part test to determine if a testator—a maker of a will—has the capacity or competency to make a will: Does the individual have sufficient mental capacity to 1) understand the nature of a will (or a testamentary act), 2) understand the nature and extent of their property, and 3) remember and understand their relationship to living descendants, their spouse, their parents, and others whose interests are affected by a will?

When it comes to the burden of proof in a capacity-related estate challenge, there is a general, rebuttable presumption that all persons have the capacity to make decisions and to be responsible for their acts or decisions. Thus the burden rests on the person challenging the will to show that the testator lacked capacity. So if a will is challenged, the capacity issue has major implications in creating a bulletproof estate plan.

Here's how lawyers look at the problem: Absent a finding of incapacity, the testator or settlor (maker of a trust) is presumed to "have the capacity to make decisions and to be responsible for their acts or decisions."[3] Capacity to make decisions is defined as:

> The ability to communicate verbally, or by any other means, the decision, and to understand and appreciate, to the extent relevant, all of the following:
>
> a) The rights, duties, and responsibilities created by or affected by the decision.
>
> b) The probable consequences for the decisionmaker and, where appropriate, the persons affected by the decision.
>
> c) The significant risks, benefit and reasonable alternatives involved in the decision.[4]

When heirs or beneficiaries approach me to look at a deceased relative's estate plan, the first part of my analysis is to decide if the testator or settlor had capacity at the time of the making of the will or trust. When a plan is being drawn up and capacity may be in doubt, some estate planners will engage psychologists, neuropsychologists, or geriatric psychiatrists—psychiatrists focused on "late-life mental health needs"[5]—to assess their client's mental capacity. These reports may be helpful in defending against estate challenges, but they are not bulletproof.

My own experience is that such efforts may simply reflect the estate planner's recognition that the estate plan is problematic and has elements likely to ignite a challenge. Disinheriting children, grossly favoring one child over another, and giving substantial assets to caregivers or recent acquaintances are all red flags of looming trouble. The drafting lawyer is a witness to his or her own efforts and in estate or trust litigation will be deposed and called as a witness at trial.

Incapacity Opens a Can of Worms

Lawyers who have drafted estate plans are often surprised that the attorney-client privilege has real limits, especially when it comes to determining whether their client was mentally competent at the time their plans were drafted. (Or, as the California Evidence Code puts it, "There is no privilege . . . as to a communication relevant to an issue between parties all of whom claim through a deceased client, regardless of whether the claims are by testate or intestate succession or by inter vivos transaction."[6]) In plain English, once the maker of a will is deceased, all parties to a litigation dispute over his or her estate can find out what the decedent told the drafting lawyer.

When appropriate, it is our practice in estate and trust litigation cases to notify the drafting attorney that he or she is a percipient witness (i.e., an eyewitness) to the litigation. Why? Because the drafter usually has an intimate and personal knowledge of the intent and mindset of the testator or settlor—often more so than any other potential witness. We ultimately ask for or subpoena time records as to meetings between the testator and the attorney, their duration, and the topics discussed.

With capacity and undue influence often at issue, we also note that the attorney's possession of confidential information regarding beneficiaries and heirs likely creates a conflict of interest and precludes the lawyer from representing the parties being sued. If the drafting lawyer insists on representing them, then we will consider filing a disqualification motion.

Capacity is not the sole factor that determines how bulletproof an estate is. The aging of the baby boomers is causing a rapid rise in America's elderly population. Since we are living longer, the incidences of aging-associated diseases are increasing rapidly. Many aging-related diseases make us more vulnerable to undue influence—not just Alzheimer's or dementia. According to the California Welfare and Institutions Code, undue influence is defined as "excessive persuasion that causes another person to act or refrain from acting by overcoming that person's free will and results in inequity."[7] Being sick, or depressed, or having any other number of common ailments in old age, can make one a target for exploitation.

The law in California is quite specific about the factors that should be considered in determining whether a result was produced by undue influence. So that you will appreciate just how specific, here's the full text of section 15610.70 of the California Welfare and Institutions Code:

(a) "Undue influence" means excessive persuasion that causes another person to act or refrain from acting by overcoming that person's free will and results in inequity. In determining whether a result was produced by undue influence, all of the following shall be considered:

(1) The vulnerability of the victim. Evidence of vulnerability may include, but is not limited to, incapacity, illness, disability, injury, age, education, impaired cognitive function, emotional distress, isolation, or dependency, and whether the influencer knew or should have known of the alleged victim's vulnerability.

(2) The influencer's apparent authority. Evidence of apparent authority may include, but is not limited to, status as a fiduciary, family member, care provider, health care professional, legal professional, spiritual adviser, expert, or other qualification.

(3) The actions or tactics used by the influencer. Evidence of actions or tactics used may include, but is not limited to, all of the following:

(A) Controlling necessaries of life, medication, the victim's interactions with others, access to information, or sleep.

(B) Use of affection, intimidation, or coercion.

(C) Initiation of changes in personal or property rights, use of haste or secrecy in effecting those changes, effecting changes at inappropriate times and places, and claims of expertise in effecting changes.

(4) The equity of the result. Evidence of the equity of the result may include, but is not limited to, the economic consequences to the victim, any divergence from the victim's prior intent or course of conduct or dealing, the relationship of the value conveyed to the value of any services or consideration received, or the appropriateness of the change in light of the length and nature of the relationship.

(b) Evidence of an inequitable result, without more, is not sufficient to prove undue influence.[8]

Here's the gist of what this all means: According to the California legislature, the vulnerability of an elder is not wholly dependent on the issue of capacity. It bears repeating: "Evidence of vulnerability may include, but is not limited to, incapacity, illness, disability, injury, age, education, impaired cognitive function, emotional distress, isolation, or dependency, and whether the influencer knew or should have known of the alleged victim's vulnerability."

The Casey Kasem Case

To understand how dementia can be used as a lever in estate contests, consider the case of the velvet voice of

American Top 40 radio, Casey Kasem. For nearly forty years, Kasem dominated the radio waves. He died from a combination of Parkinson's, dementia, and other medical problems, at the age of eighty-two.

Kasem's first marriage, in 1972, ended in divorce but produced three children, Mike, Julie, and Kerri. In 1980, he married the actress Jean Thompson and had one more child, Liberty Jean. In 2007, Kasem was diagnosed with Parkinson's and, a few months later, he was further diagnosed with Lewy body dementia. He retired from public life in 2009, and from that point on his health became progressively worse.

Kasem was extremely wealthy and had hired top lawyers to draft all the requisite legal documents for his estate. He had a will and had set up trusts for his family, all of which any competent attorney would recommend to someone in his position. But from the moment he was diagnosed with dementia, his estate became vulnerable.

In 2013, Kasem's wife placed him in a hospital—and the fighting over his estimated $80 million estate kicked off. The relationship between the stepmother and the stepchildren became more strained once Kasem was under hospital care. *The Hollywood Reporter* found out that Kasem's children from his first marriage did not even know Kasem was hospitalized until he had already been there a week, and visits to see him were restricted by Jean Thompson Kasem.[9] Then the legal battles began. His daughter Julie filed a lawsuit against her stepmother in superior court seeking temporary appointment of conservatorship over her father. According to the gossip site TMZ, Julie alleged that her father had:

- major impairment to short term, long term, and immediate recall memory

- major impairment to verbally communicate [sic]

- major impairment to perform simple calculations, plan simple tasks, and reason logically [sic]

- severely disorganized thinking

- moderate hallucinations[10]

The suit alleged that Kasem was grossly mistreated once he became mentally impaired and that Jean Thompson Kasem was responsible.

The case was ultimately denied with prejudice in 2014, meaning the same issues raised in the lawsuit could not be argued any further. But a new case petition was brought in May of that year, at which point a different court and judge granted temporary guardianship to Kasem's children. The drama escalated further when the children tried to get sheriffs to transport Casey Kasem to an emergency room. Doctors, lawyers, and court-appointed representatives wrangled back and forth for weeks. Ultimately, her step-children alleged that Jean Thompson Kasem should have been prosecuted for abuse.

The story does not have a happier ending, unfortunately. Kasem's wife was unable to regain custody, and Kasem's condition worsened in the hospital. On June 14, 2014, medical care was withdrawn, and Kasem died a few hours later. The legal case escalated; Jean Thompson Kasem filed a lawsuit against her stepchildren claiming wrongful death, and the battle over his estate began.

So was Casey Kasem the victim of elder abuse? Did his second wife hasten his demise, either intentionally or through neglect? Or did something else happen? The answers are more elusive than you might expect. Untangling the facts from the emotion and sequence of events will be difficult. Six years later, doctors and lawyers are still arguing over Kasem's estate, and they may yet be doing so for much longer.

If someone had come to me for advice about this situation in 2013, I would have asked both the stepmother and the stepchildren to establish a dialogue, to talk about the hard issues that would arise ahead, and to establish a way to take care of their ailing father/husband first, and then protect the assets he accrued over a lifetime of hard work. Direct communication between the parties is crucial, or else everyone ends up communicating through lawyers, which is exactly what happened here.

Why Estate Plans Often Fail

I listen to hundreds of stories every year. Many of the hundreds of short videos we've created for HackardLaw.com end with a sentence or two that invites storytelling and provides our phone number for those who would like to call us: "If you have an elder financial abuse matter that you would like to talk about"; "If you want to share your story and see if we can help"; "If you would like to talk with Hackard Law about your case, call us today at . . ." There are dozens of stories for every element of vulnerability. The stories surrounding each element often provide a foundation for the failure of an estate plan that someone tried to make bulletproof.

So what kind of stories do I hear about capacity and the other elements of an undue influence claim? Let's start with capacity, which is where estate and trust litigators look first. For wills, the standard questions are whether the individual had sufficient mental capacity to be able to understand the testamentary act, the nature of their property, and their relations to their family. I hear plenty of stories where the individual thinks that their long-deceased spouse is living, their children go unrecognized, or there is little self-awareness. Delusions and hallucinations of all kinds may abound.

Illness, disability, injury, age, education, impaired cognitive function, emotional distress, isolation, or dependency are other factors used to evaluate undue influence. Wrongdoers regularly isolate their victims: cut off their telephones, prevent entry into the elder's house, use baby monitors to spy on their conversations, and threaten catastrophe if the isolation is pierced.

Dependency is one of the most common factors. It's in this situation that the tables can turn. A jobless substance abuser—most often a child or grandchild—is often a longtime resident of an elder's home. Lacking independent financial means, the abuser lives off the elder, taking food and shelter without compensation. As the elder ages, they become more dependent on the person who is financially dependent on them. Given the elder's dependence, a wrongdoer can threaten the loss of home or freedom if they are not given the elder's house, other assets, or entire estate. Unfortunately, this happens with regularity.

Don't Fool Yourself: No Plan Is Foolproof

Let's go back to the original question posed: "Why aren't estates bulletproof?" In short, we are all human, and we are therefore all fallible. Experience, scripture, and classic literature lead us to the same conclusion. The parable of the rich fool (Luke 12:13–21) can tell us a lot about the assumptions that we make in planning:

Someone in the crowd said to him, "Teacher, tell my brother to divide the inheritance with me." Jesus replied, "Man, who appointed me a judge or an arbiter between you?" Then he said to them, "Watch out! Be on your guard against all kinds of greed; life does not consist in an abundance of possessions."

And he told them this parable:

"The ground of a certain rich man yielded an abundant harvest. He thought to himself, 'What shall I do? I have no place to store my crops.'

"Then he said, 'This is what I'll do. I will tear down my barns and build bigger ones, and there I will store my surplus grain.'

'And I'll say to myself, "You have plenty of grain laid up for many years. Take life easy; eat, drink and be merry."

"But God said to him, 'You fool! This very night your life will be demanded from you. Then who will get what you have prepared for yourself?'

"This is how it will be with whoever stores up things for themselves but is not rich toward God."

That which we store up for ourselves does not last.

I was recently reviewing draft information for a Form 706, otherwise known as a United States Estate (and Generation-Skipping Transfer) Tax Return. These returns must be filed (by an executor) for individuals who died in 2018 and whose gross estate plus the adjusted taxable gifts they received during their lifetime are valued at more than $11,180,000. The estate of the individual whose Form 706 draft I was reviewing was far more than the $11 million threshold. I assume that the decedent was proud of her accumulated and extensive wealth, which was all listed in

Part 5 of the form and its schedules. Amidst the tens of millions of dollars' worth of listed assets, there was a small section for deductions—specifically, "Schedule J–Funeral Expenses and Expenses Incurred in Administering Property Subject to Claims." It was the draft information for that schedule that struck me: "Family Cremation" ($2,100.00) and "Ashes Containers" ($510.00).

These brief line items illustrate the larger picture: Our lives and our estates are not bulletproof. Nothing lasts forever. I've litigated a multitude of estate and trust lawsuits that challenged others' efforts to bulletproof their own interests. Some challenges are very sad, and few are happy. More than once have clients concluded at the end of a long, painful process that, in the words of Jesus's parable, "Life does not consist of an abundance of possessions."

The importance of family and caring becomes even more evident in the stark context of estate disputes. Ultimately, I hope we see that for the sake of happiness and a strong sense of gratitude, there are more important things than bulletproofing our estates. This is the very lesson in Dickens's *A Christmas Carol*. After his frightened contemplation of his past, present, and future, Scrooge becomes a changed man:

> Scrooge was better than his word. He did it all, and infinitely more; and to Tiny Tim, who did not die, he was a second father. He became as good a friend, as good a master, and as good a man, as the good old city knew, or any other good old city, town, or borough, in the good old world. Some people laughed to see the alteration in him, but he let them laugh, and little heeded them; for he was wise enough to know that nothing ever happened on this globe, for good, at which some people did not have their fill of laughter in the outset; and knowing that such as these would be blind anyway, he thought it quite as well that they should wrinkle up their eyes in grins, as have the

malady in less attractive forms. His own heart laughed: and that was quite enough for him.[11]

We all seek certainty. We all look for safety in the face of risks. But it's a fool's errand. Life is full of risks, and the elimination of all of them is impossible. We transport ourselves across town or country in vehicles or planes that can break down or fail. We eat food and drink beverages that are considered by some to be beneficial in extending life and by others as harmful and likely to lead to an early death. We face unexpected setbacks: natural disasters, health problems, economic collapse—the list is endless.

Here, then, is the bottom line: If you want precise things to happen systematically after you die, you will need to hire a professional with *profound* experience, knowledge, and judgment. Even then, you should know that hiring even the top lawyer of all time is no guarantee that your best-laid plans won't go awry. This does not mean that you should give up and avoid the whole exercise. Quite the contrary; a fair plan created by an average professional will be far better than no plan at all.

My advice? Plan for the best but expect the worst.

The Widowed Stepmother

When US senator and Hollywood actor Fred Thompson died in November of 2015 at the age of seventy-three, he left behind a rich legacy in both politics and show business. Not only had Thompson represented his home state of Tennessee in the senate from 1993 to 2004, his strong jaw and good-old-boy charisma had become familiar to anyone who watched *Law & Order* or any number of political thrillers. After his passing, though, a different kind of drama unfolded. A familiar dispute erupted, one that has led to contentious litigation over his estate.

Thompson had been married twice, bringing up two children with each of his wives. As is typical in these situations, after his death a fight over the estate's assets broke out between the children from his first marriage and their stepmother, and the case ended up in probate court. Tony and Dan Thompson, the late senator's sons from his first marriage, filed an action alleging undue influence over the ailing Thompson by his second wife, Jeri, in his final days.[1] Fred and Jeri Thompson had married in 2002, producing a daughter a year later and a son in 2006. (Jeri was twenty-four years his junior.) She had been designated the primary beneficiary of her husband's estate, from which $50,000 each was allotted to Tony and Dan by their father.

Jeri Thompson, however, decided to fight back against her stepsons' claims that they did not receive enough, stating that no changes to the will were made that concerned Tony and Dan's inheritance in the estate. Her legal team unloaded on the two elder Thompson sons, and she pushed to have the lawsuit dismissed. The motion she filed made her position abundantly clear:

> Each of [Thompson's sons'] alleged claims against [Jeri Thompson] in this matter is founded upon a single premise - that [Jeri Thompson] took something that belonged to [Thompson's sons] either through her own actions or by influencing the actions of Senator Thompson. That premise is unsound, unsupported and contradicted by the undisputed facts of this case. No person made any changes to Senator Thompson's estate plans in October 2015 that caused any change in [Thompson's sons'] position.[2]

Jeri's legal team went on to argue that aside from provisions made for the two younger Thompson children, no changes to the will were made. His sons from his first marriage were concerned over the fact that Thompson had hired attorneys to make changes to his will in the months before his death; his condition worsened, however, and his attorneys concluded that he no longer had the capacity for such decisions, and thus, no changes were implemented. For the elder Thompson sons, the key to proving undue influence might have been found in the circumstances surrounding his last actual change to the will. They didn't find any, however. In March of 2017, Tony and Dan threw in the proverbial towel, stating, "The discovery documents we saw satisfied us that our father's final wishes were followed, allowing us to dismiss the lawsuit."[3]

Whether an estate case involves celebrities, politicians, or normal everyday folks, there is no escaping human nature. The fact is, the potential for estate and trust litigation grows whenever there's an uneasy relationship between a stepmother and children from a first marriage. Fred Thompson's legacy proved to be no exception.

The Curious Case of Alan Thicke

He was born Alan Willis Jeffrey in Ontario, Canada, in 1947, but we remember him by his stage name, Alan Thicke—a popular comedian, talk show host, and actor best known for his role as Dr. Jason Seaver on the '80s sitcom *Growing Pains*.

Thicke was married three times and the father of three sons, two by his first marriage and one by his second. It was his third marriage, to Tanya Callau, a model he married in 2005, that ultimately led to a legal battle over the late actor's estate when he died in 2016. At sixty-nine years old, he had a heart attack while playing ice hockey with his adult son Carter.

Unlike most celebrities who remarry a second or third time, Thicke took steps to protect his assets for his children by requiring Callau to sign a prenuptial agreement four days before they wed. But as often happens in families with widowed stepmothers, two of Thicke's sons—including singer, songwriter, and producer Robin Thicke—feared that their stepmother would seize control of their father's estate.

Six months after Thicke died, disputes escalated over the $16 million estate. In May 2018, Callau filed court documents claiming that her stepsons were withholding her rightful inheritance and were charging her for taxes and other expenses. The sons, in turn, filed a lawsuit claiming that Callau wanted to overturn the prenuptial agreement she had with Alan Thicke in order to inherit a disproportionate amount of his estate.

That preemptive strike to sue their stepmother over allegations that she was planning to challenge the prenup ended up backfiring. The judge in the case said that there was no evidence that Callau planned to sue over Thicke's will and no evidence that she wanted to challenge the agreement. Once the judge overturned the brothers' petition, a settlement in the case was quickly reached.[4]

In the end, Callau received 40 percent of the estate, up from the original 25 percent stipulated in Thicke's will, while each of Thicke's three sons received 20 percent. Callau also was allowed to remain at her late husband's Carpinteria, California, ranch for the remainder of her life, provided she maintains the property.

Callau said she harbors no ill will towards her stepsons. After the judge's ruling she wrote on Instagram: "Judge threw out my stepsons [sic] lawsuit. Reality check ...... I only wish them the best and may we all start healing."[5]

While this case appears to have been settled amicably, it is yet another example of how the best-laid plans to avoid an estate battle in a blended family go awry. So don't be tempted to think the stars are better off than the rest of us in any essential way. Fame and fortune only seem to magnify the misery of a family feud.

Why Are There So Many Stepmother Problems?

The stories of Fred Thompson, Alan Thicke, and Tony Curtis (from Chapter 2) are just three high-profile estate dispute cases involving stepmothers and children from earlier marriages, but they are certainly not the exception. Perhaps it's just human nature, but speaking as an estate lawyer with over forty years of legal experience, I think it's fair to say that nearly every time there is a stepmother and children from an earlier marriage there will be friction between family members after the father dies. And when assets and estates are larger, the chance of litigation or dispute grows in direct relation to their size.

Here's a situation I see at my firm on a regular basis: A father dies. The stepmother is appointed as trustee of her husband's trust, while the adult children from a previous marriage are designated as beneficiaries of their father's trust. The stepmother and stepchildren have always had a chilly relationship. Conflict ensues.

When you introduce trust funds or other estate assets into such a volatile mix, chances are high for conflict. Going to court for trust or probate litigation is not at all unexpected.

It's not all doom and gloom, however. If you can spot the red flags that signal family estate fights ahead, you can save yourself time, money, and the emotional stress that comes with litigation. Think of litigation as fighting a fire. The firefighters arrive on the scene when a house is in flames. In the same way, my litigation team can respond quickly to a conflict to safeguard clients and their assets. But the best strategy for defending an estate is to prevent conflicts before they break out, much like the best way to prevent a fire is to stop it from ever starting.

I was recently contacted by Next Avenue, an excellent nonprofit news resource for American seniors that is produced by Twin Cities PBS. Next Avenue had heard about my 2017 book *The Wolf at the Door: Undue Influence and Elder Financial Abuse* and asked if they could reprint an excerpt of it on their site. The topic they chose to excerpt? The role of stepmothers in disputed estates, which they chose because it is rapidly becoming the number one source of conflict in estate and probate matters.

Before I continue, I'd like to assert that I certainly don't think stepmothers are inherently bad or in the wrong. I simply seek to point out that the likelihood of conflict between stepmothers and stepchildren over estate and trust assets is fairly high.[6] Very often, family dynamics, social realities, and other circumstances conspire to place stepmothers and biological children on a collision course.

Demographic data confirms what a trust litigator knows from experience about stepmother cases. Each of these figures helps us gain a clearer perspective on the problem:

- The average life expectancy for women in the United States is 81.2 years on average, versus 76.4 years for men, making for a much higher population of widows than widowers.[7]

- There are currently seventy-five million baby boomers in the United States (sixty-five million of whom were born here); one in eight Americans, or forty million people, are over the age of sixty-five. Ten thousand baby boomers turn sixty-five every day.[8]

- Chances of cognitive decline from diseases like dementia and Alzheimer's increase drastically with

age between sixty-five and ninety, doubling approx-
imately every five years.[9]

Add in enough assets and a turbulent family history, and
you've got a ready-made recipe for a raucous estate battle.
The fact is, the challenges posed by elder financial abuse
and undue influence aren't going away, and blended families are at special risk for disaster.

While it's clear that we have an aging population in the
United States, and that women outlive men, what's less obvious are all the reasons why stepmother issues in estates
are likely to become the fastest-growing area of estate litigation. Simply put, adverse family dynamics are at the
heart of the issue.

Consider these startling facts about blended families:

- Only 20 percent of adult stepchildren feel close to
  their stepmothers.

- Parents with stepchildren are 30 to 35 percent more
  likely to make unequal bequests. Why? The main
  factors include:

  o **Long-term co-residence.** Whoever lives
    with the parent the longest usually gets the
    greater bequest.

  o **No or little contact.** Whoever has the least
    contact with the parent usually gets the lesser
    bequest.

  o **Geography.** Whoever lives the farthest away
    usually gets the lesser bequest.

- Parents with wills are 33 percent more likely to make unequal bequests.[10]

In February 2018, *TheStreet* published a provocative article titled "My Stepmother Stole My Inheritance" by business and finance writer Brian O'Connell. The article quotes a number of authors (myself included) as it explores the idea that the "issue of warring stepfamilies after the main breadwinner passes is generating some heat in estate inheritance circles, as adult children accuse step-spouses of grabbing the lion's share of the estate."[11]

How Can We Stop the (Un)Civil Wars?

Let's step back for a minute and think about what, at least in part, is going on between stepmothers and their stepchildren in the scenarios I've discussed above. When it comes to stepmother battles, it's helpful to acknowledge the father's biological children as the first generation of his family. The children in this first generation, even if their family thread is severed by their parents' divorce, have certain expectations of what is due to them.

The husband's second marriage fractures this inheritance expectation. The stepmother supplants the role of the husband's biological children—a role focused on entrenchment, the preservation of financial success coupled with the fear of losing what has already been received.

The biological children's generational displacement carries with it a questioning of identity, of belonging. "I am my father's child. He worked hard for his wealth. My stepmother didn't earn a bit of what my father created. She divided our family. Now she's taking its wealth and destroying our heritage," is a common refrain. I've found the outrage and sense of injustice is inversely proportional to the length of the second marriage.

If you are a stepmother and are reading this book, you may be wondering if there is anything you can do to avoid a future (or current) problem with your stepchildren. Indeed, there is! The number one piece of advice I want to give you is to engage in a healthy dialogue with your stepchildren. Listen to their concerns, acknowledge their anxieties, and understand where they are coming from. You will never be able to reach any agreement with them unless they feel their issues, concerns, or problems have been heard and understood. If it's not possible to have such a constructive conversation without drama or animosity, you may need to have a friend or an independent mediator help facilitate the dialogue.

If you're an adult child with a stepmother and *you're* reading this book, here are some suggestions for you to consider as well. As noted above, my number one piece of advice is to engage in a healthy dialogue with your stepmother. If your father is still alive, it can be beneficial to discuss his estate plans with him. His primary concern will often be the reasonable allocation of income to his spouse after his passing. The mechanics of trust planning can help ensure your surviving stepmother continues to receive an income, while at the same time preserving (and possibly distributing) some assets to you and your siblings. Your stepmother should be a part of this planning process. Note, however, that to the extent that she has community property assets, such assets are basically "off the table" for further discussion.

Disagreements are typical, but it should be noted that only a fraction of estate settlements with surviving stepmothers actually devolve into litigation. Factors that are more likely to ignite such litigation include:

- brief marriages

- large separate property assets with a smaller proportion of community property assets

- estate changes that are made while the husband lacks capacity or is vulnerable to undue influence

- isolation of the husband by the stepmother from his biological children

When these fights ignite, it helps to have experienced counsel on both sides of the conflict—counsel who know the battleground and the peace processes that can move litigants toward a less painful resolution. An "all or nothing" approach on either side is often a path to disaster.

When it comes down to it, stepmothers and their stepchildren are family—a family with conflict, but a family nonetheless. The plaintive words of Abraham Lincoln's First Inaugural Address, delivered on the eve of our nation's civil war, ring true in fights within all families: "Though passion may have strained, it must not break our bonds of affection. The mystic chords of memory will swell when again touched, as surely they will be, by the better angels of our nature."[12]

Four years after Lincoln's "better angels" speech, he reflected on how "the war came" and went, and that "[n]either party expected . . . the magnitude, or the duration [of the war]. . . . Each looked for an easier triumph, and a result less fundamental and astounding."[13]

Family estate fights can truly feel like civil war. The human and financial costs of the fight can result in unexpected and astounding changes. As counsel, often our role in estate litigation is to prevent a "runaway train"—a protracted process driven by emotion, devoid of practicality, and lacking human decency.

In each of these conflicts, my sincere hope is that at some point in the litigation the parties will focus more on resolution than contention. While an attempted resolution is not always successful, it is always surely worth the effort.

Problem Trustee Removal

Her name was Margaret, and I was meeting her for the first time in my office conference room in Mather, California. She was in her mid-sixties, well-dressed, with gray hair pulled back in a bun and sensible shoes.

"Mr. Hackard, I don't want to take up too much of your time, so I'll come straight to the point," she said with great precision. "My older brother, Stanley, is the executor of my parents' trust. For the past two years, since our parents died, he has been systematically selling off assets and using the proceeds to gamble. Is there any way to stop him before there's nothing left of the estate?"

Every profession has words or expressions peculiar to it. The meaning of these words may be familiar to those inside the profession but be baffling to or misunderstood by an outsider. I think that this is especially true with the word "trustee." Estate and trust lawyers use the word every day. Those outside the profession don't.

I hear so often from heirs or trust beneficiaries, like Margaret, that they or someone else is the "executor" of the trust. It takes a little more listening to figure out what is really being said.

An "executor" is the person named in a decedent's will to be appointed by the probate court as the personal representative of the estate.[1] A trustee, on the other hand, is a person or entity that has the power to collect, hold, and retain trust property received from a settlor (the maker of a trust). A trustee's powers and duties are defined in the trust itself and in the law. Stanley, as it turns out, was actually a trustee.

Trust beneficiaries call us to ask about their rights in a trust and how the obligations and actions of a trustee affect those rights. The questions often stem from a perceived error, malfeasance, or inaction on the trustee's part. To give you a sense of why these questions of concern are so common, let's start from the beginning and go over some of the common ways trustees are selected.

Well-meaning parents frequently set up living trusts for their children decades before they end up passing away. In most cases, the named trustees are the parents themselves and then, in order, their children, oldest to youngest. At some point the father or mother dies, leaving the other parent in charge of the trust. With a massive sigh of relief, the surviving husband or wife realizes that the trust document saved them from having to endure a lengthy probate proceeding, and so they decide to "leave well enough alone." What happens next is highly predictable: A few years later, the surviving spouse dies, leaving the eldest child as the trustee.

The story would have a happy ending, except that the eldest child may be entirely unfit or unsuitable to take over the financial affairs of the deceased parents—just like

Margaret's brother, Stanley. Addictions of all kinds lead to problems with trustees, and the most common addictions of all in such cases are drugs and alcohol.

Drugs and Alcohol Addiction in Trust Contests

Our families are at risk from those who abuse drugs and alcohol. In California more than one-third of traffic deaths involve a drunk driver,[2] and more than 25 percent of crash fatalities are drug-involved.[3] Eighty-one percent of arrests in Sacramento involve people who have tested positive for illegal drug use.[4]

When it comes to trusts and estates, substance abuse can cause the disposition of family assets to go in unexpected and distressing directions. The potential for painful drama often begins when a problem child—rather, an adult, unemployed and living with an elder parent—begins to take hold of their parent's finances. Dangerous implications follow. A parent's savings may be drained, and deep family divisions may occur as an elderly parent is frozen out from communicating with their other children. Bank accounts are changed to provide access to the abusive child. Often a power of attorney is given to the child—a sure invitation to raid the cookie jar.

A problem-child substance abuser may not be the figure who ruins a parent's estate, but regardless of the perpetrator, the pattern is the same. They'll take the parent to an unwitting or deceived attorney to change the parent's estate plan. Most changes involve replacing a responsible trustee or successor trustee (i.e., replacement trustee) with the problem child. They may also change the parent's beneficiary designations—the house now goes to the problem child; maybe everything does—but at the very least, the problem child gets an inordinate share of the estate.[5]

Signs of financial wrongdoing by the alcohol or substance abuser may become clear only after the parent's death. This is when beneficiaries realize the house was transferred to the wrongdoer before the parent's death, the bank accounts are depleted, and a new will or trust is in place. Secrecy hid their wrongdoing.

It takes experience to solve the puzzle of rights and remedies in a contested probate, estate, or trust case. Legally and morally, an elder has a right to be free of physical and financial coercion. This right is enforced after the discovery of wrongdoing—which, unfortunately, too often occurs after the elder's death.

The remedy for wrongdoing is to hold the wrongdoer responsible. Judicial resources must be employed to right the wrong. Experienced legal counsel will explore the costs and benefits of litigation and identify other acceptable legal remedies available to wronged heirs and beneficiaries.

Issues Leading to Trust Contests

In my experience, here are the ten most common causes of why someone may be unfit to manage a trust, in order of frequency:

1. Substance abuse—i.e., a relative who is addicted to alcohol or drugs
2. Gambling addiction
3. Mental instability
4. Severe physical incapacity
5. A lack of interest in managing a trust
6. Financial distress, which could lead to self-dealing

7.   Neglecting trust duties, perhaps due to being too busy
8.   An inability to get along with trust beneficiaries
9.   Inexperience in managing any financial affairs
10. An unwillingness to comply with explicit trust conditions

The above list, while certainly not exhaustive, shows that managing a trust, even in the best of circumstances, is no easy matter, and there are a multitude of ways in which things can go wrong. As Murphy's Law clearly states, things will go wrong—and at the very worst time.

Removing a Named Trustee Is Not Impossible

Many people wrongly assume that a named trustee, often a sibling, cannot be removed from their position. In fact, even trained litigators sometimes don't understand why and how to remove someone as trustee. I have personally witnessed many cases where an attorney filed a lawsuit in superior court as a way of removing a problem trustee, which is akin to using a sledgehammer to drive a nail. Perhaps that may be one way of trying to solve the problem, but there are better, more efficient, and less expensive ways. Attorneys who don't understand the nuances of probate, trust, and estate law are likely to make costly mistakes that ultimately hurt their client.

My firm regularly represents clients in trust, estate, and probate litigation and is often called upon to enforce a wronged beneficiary's right to an accounting from an uncommunicative, recalcitrant, or duplicitous trustee.[6] While California probate courts will follow the law and order a trustee to provide an accounting, this is only part of what is often necessary to safeguard the beneficiary's trust interests and to prevent further harm to an innocent beneficiary.

A trustee's refusal to make trust distributions is one of the most common reasons for filing a petition for a court-ordered accounting. Waiting on an inheritance is a continual source of frustration to estate and trust heirs or beneficiaries. As noted earlier, trustee inaction may stem from sheer incompetence, inexperience, poor counsel, mismanagement, laziness, or the simple desire to be in control and stay in control. Whether the reasons for the failure to distribute the inheritance are wrongful, negligent, or innocent, the delay must be addressed.

"To start the process of removing a trustee, " I explained to Margaret, "you must first review all documents (the will, revocable or irrevocable trust, insurance, and IRA beneficiary designations), prepare timelines, and make a list of interested parties. All of this helps to focus on the reasons for the trustee's failure to do their job."[7]

In California, an essential part of dealing with a problem trustee is to understand that the trustee wields a great deal of power. Statutory rules governing trustee authority and power are uniform statewide, though there are slight variations in local courts.[8] Local rules must be reviewed and understood when it comes to challenging a trustee's actions, as the local probate rules in San Francisco will be different than those of San Diego, Los Angeles, or Sacramento.

A trustee's job is to marshal or collect assets, communicate with creditors, and distribute assets or income to beneficiaries in accord with the trust's terms. It is not at all unusual that a trustee favors himself or someone else as a beneficiary, attempts to sell trust assets to a favored person at a discount, or freezes some beneficiaries out of income and information.

Nevertheless, there is often sufficient information to support the suspension or removal of a trustee. Courts will move to protect beneficiaries and do not take their responsibility lightly. Many people assume that it is extremely difficult or even nearly impossible to remove a trustee, but that is not the case. In Margaret's situation, where her older brother had a serious and documented gambling problem, a court replaced him in a matter of days.

The key in this and all other cases of trustee removal is due diligence and a thorough review of the trust. Of course, sometimes this is not possible, since part of the trustee's wrongdoing or misdeeds may include failing to provide a beneficiary or heir with a copy of the trust.

The ultimate public policy behind California's trustee laws is the preservation of the trust property. California Probate Code Section 15642 delineates some of the reasons supporting removal, explaining that:

(a) A trustee may be removed in accordance with the trust instrument, by the court on its own motion, or on petition of a settlor, cotrustee, or beneficiary under Section 17200.

(b) The grounds for removal of a trustee by the court include the following:

(1) Where the trustee has committed a breach of the trust.

(2) Where the trustee is insolvent or otherwise unfit to administer the trust.

(3) Where hostility or lack of cooperation among cotrustees impairs the administration of the trust.

(4) Where the trustee fails or declines to act.

(5) Where the trustee's compensation is excessive under the circumstances.

Forcing the Issue

Trust, probate, and estate litigators will often seek an early suspension of the existing trustee's powers and the appointment of a temporary trustee.[9] These initial actions are frequently done on an expedited or "ex parte" basis (i.e., representing one side only) to preserve the trust, with the understanding that allegations of wrongdoing will be proven or disproven at a later hearing. While these early suspension efforts are paid for by the challenging beneficiaries, such challenges usually include a request that the probate court judge not use trust assets to pay for the defense's legal counsel. This can be a major point of contention.

Recent Judicial Council of California court statistics confirm that just in Los Angeles alone, probate and mental-health court trials total more than 14,000 per year.[10] Many of these trials involve beneficiaries alleging wrongdoing against a trustee or battles to remove an existing trustee.

What's the background that sets the stage for all of these trustee disputes in LA? We start by noting that a living trust becomes irrevocable at the death or incapacity of its maker.[11] New trustees are often appointed when the trust becomes irrevocable or when conflicts arise between a beneficiary and the trustee.[12] Disputes between former trustees and new or successor trustees often occur when the successor trustee requests some, if not all, documents held by the former trustee or the former trustee's attorney.

A California court of appeal recently addressed this issue in *Fiduciary Trust International of California v. Klein*

(2017). The lessons of the Klein decision are worth discussing, and include the findings that: a) Whether a trustee was removed by court order or voluntarily resigns, attorney-client privilege protects the client; b) the client is considered to be the office of the trustee rather than a particular trustee; c) a trustee must preserve trust property; and d) such property includes the trust's legal files.[13]

The power to assert confidential communications privilege (aka attorney-client privilege) moves to the successor trustee.[14] If this were not so, the successor trustee would not be unable to do their job in protecting and preserving trust property.[15] A predecessor trustee should not be allowed to interfere with or prevent the transfer of attorney-client trust files to the new trustee.

The very narrow exception to this rule is when a predecessor trustee distinguishes, scrupulously and painstakingly, his or her own interests from those of the beneficiaries of the trust. Moreover, a California appellate court case notes that if a predecessor trustee seeks legal advice in his own personal capacity (not in his capacity as a trustee) and pays for the advice out of his own private funds, he may be able (not *shall* be able) to avoid disclosing the advice to a successor trustee.[16]

Before contacting a lawyer and going down this road, you should clearly understand that trustee succession battles can be brutal.[17] You should also be aware that the discovery process to obtain legal files and attorney-client communications with the predecessor trustee can be protracted.

That said, the Klein case gives guidance and hope to those successor trustees who require the trust's legal files to protect trust assets and prevent any further harm to trust beneficiaries.[18] The good news is that the law provides for a clear path when incompetent, unethical, incapacitated, and/or neglectful trustees must be removed.

Unequal Inheritance: Siblings and Half-Siblings

I magine you're an attorney and you're sitting in one of the probate divisions of the superior court in one of California's fifty-eight counties, waiting for your client's matter to be called. Today you may be representing the wronged beneficiary of a trust, a challenged trustee, a disinherited heir, or an executor attempting to keep a will valid.

You know that history repeats itself with regularity in the state's probate dockets. The couple to your right is whispering that a stepsister is only in court to get her stepfather's money. The middle-aged man to your left is busy writing notes to his lawyer about his half-sister's efforts to freeze him out of his mother's estate. Attorneys at the counsel tables are arguing over whether a decedent's stepson was a valid beneficiary in a trust. Attorneys in the previous matter heard before the court, which involved the transfer of an eighty-three-year-old elder's house to his unemployed alcoholic daughter just weeks before his death, are now out in the hall trying to settle the case.

Those new to these dockets may wonder whether any families actually have estate plans that *do* work without bickering and challenge. As an estate litigator and probate attorney, I meet many clients who express shock and consternation at the seeming necessity of estate litigation. Perhaps, but in the idiom of the day, "It is what it is." At times we feel like trauma center physicians who wish that everyone drove sober but must put these thoughts aside and deal with the emergency at hand.

I see the same mistakes, estate battles, and family drama again and again, and I'm a firm believer that categorizing some of these repetitive issues can help identify problems early on (and maybe even fix them). Disinterested observations about trusts and estates with heirs who include siblings, stepsiblings, half-siblings, and/or stepparents are useful. They are not intended to stereotype or imply that all families with stepparents and stepchildren are destined for probate disputes—or, for that matter, that all families without stepchildren or stepparents can expect trust and estate administration to be simple, straightforward, and guided by familial cooperation and understanding.

But as I've mentioned in previous chapters, unfortunately the chances for a family feud in estate matters increase with blended families—and blended families are on the rise across the United States. One out of every two marriages in this country ends in divorce, and it's likely there are now more stepfamilies than original families. Leaving aside the whole demographic issue, is it any wonder that estate disputes are becoming more and more common?

The Jerry Lee Lewis Case

Just down the street from Scott's Pharmacy and the Sevier Memorial United Methodist Church in Ferriday, Louisiana, and near a big dusty farm, you'll find a newly christened street called Jerry Lee Lewis Avenue, named after the town's favorite son. Although Lewis is best known for a string of rock 'n' roll hits including "Great Balls of Fire," in 2017, he became famous for something else: being an alleged victim of elder financial abuse.

At eighty-three, Lewis doesn't perform as often, but he still has a loyal following and is a beloved entertainer. So how does someone go from being an international celebrity and rock 'n' roll legend to becoming a potential victim of elder financial abuse? It turns out that even if you're rich and famous, having a turbulent personal life in your younger years often leads to a turbulent family life later on.

Lewis has been married seven times, most recently in 2012, and he has a total of six children. The daughter of his third wife, Phoebe, was Lewis's manager from 2000 until, not coincidentally, 2012. Lewis's newest wife, Judith, did not get along with her new stepdaughter, and that ultimately led to a lawsuit being filed in 2017 against both Phoebe (and her husband) for defamation, elder financial abuse, and fraud.

Among other things, Jerry Lee Lewis and his current wife claimed his daughter spent $5 million of Lewis's money on cars, real estate, and plastic surgery while plying the singer with drugs and keeping him in a moldy house that was so toxic he resorted to wearing an oxygen mask.

That initial lawsuit was dismissed for being filed in the wrong state, but it was subsequently refiled, after which Lewis's daughter countered with a lawsuit of her own against her stepmother. Phoebe Lewis-Loftin claimed

Judith had been increasing the dosages of opiates given to Lewis, causing him to become incoherent and wheelchair-bound. She asked a court to order psychological tests to establish whether Lewis does or does not have the capacity to make decisions.

As these things go, when families go to war over assets, it quickly gets complicated. The drama surrounding the Lewis family continues to play out in courtrooms in Mississippi, where he currently resides, and it may be years before the cases will be settled. In the meantime, we are left with more questions than answers. Did Lewis's daughter take financial advantage of her aging father? Was Lewis medically mistreated? Does Lewis have the capacity to make good financial decisions, or is he being manipulated by those around him? Separating fact from fiction will take some real work.

Regardless of what happens, the cases are already shaping up to be a sad and unnecessary end to what has been an epic musical career. How could this have been avoided?

Relationships between stepmothers and stepchildren will always be challenging, but they don't need to result in acrimony, anger, and animosity. Reputations and relationships, carefully built and nurtured for decades, can crumble in days. There are better ways; there are better choices.

When it comes to tensions between stepchildren and stepmothers, resolution starts with communication. At the point when Lewis was about to marry his seventh wife, there needed to be some serious, honest conversations about Lewis's health, finances, stability, goals, and ongoing relationships with his family. For the Lewis family's relationships to deteriorate so badly that they ended in courtroom accusations of elder financial abuse and fraud five years later, such conversations must not have happened.

The Eight Faces of Estate Challengers

The Jerry Lee Lewis case highlights patterns I've noticed in my own practice. In my experience, certain types of family members are more likely to cause an estate to end up in court. Any one of these kinds of siblings, stepsiblings, or half-siblings can create the right conditions for acrimony, disagreement, and, ultimately, litigation, but some families are unlucky enough to have more than one! If you recognize these faces in your own family, be aware that your chances of having to find a legal solution to your problems may greatly increase. Let's run through them:

The Serial Litigator

Oftentimes a family will have a member or spouse of a member who is proud of filing lawsuits and settling or winning them. Perhaps they've sued various small businesses in town over minor issues. They even brag how they sued the city and won after tripping over an uneven sidewalk. Hitting others with meaningless lawsuits is a game they enjoy, and this family member is not above (or below) taking stepbrothers, stepsisters, or even their own siblings and parents to court for another miserable round of estate litigation. A Serial Litigator can be a real threat to an estate— particularly one who is indifferent to the reality that most of the estate assets may wind up being consumed by attorneys' fees. The Serial Litigator's indifference may have little consequence to them but devastating financial consequences to their relatives.

The Unpopular Stepmother

First off, as noted in Chapter 5, I don't mean to imply that any "evil stepmother" stereotype so common in fairy tales applies to probate litigation. Rather, my observation is simply that during my long career, I have frequently witnessed conflicts in estate matters between stepmothers and stepchildren. We've represented both sides, and we've seen how tensions in blended families can carry over into disputes over an inheritance, beneficiary rights to a trust, estate property, etc. At times there are even accusations of fraud and undue influence—claims of a validity to be determined through discovery in court. Stepmothers who have not built solid relationships with their stepchildren while the husband/father was still living are often destined to see those children in court. The sad truth is that stepchildren who don't like or get along with their stepmother are more likely to find reasons to fight for Dad's estate, whether or not there's a case. Call it human nature—we just don't want people we don't like to win.

The Amateur Google Legal Expert

We know how beneficial the internet can be when it comes to solving all manner of problems, from simple home repair issues to basic language translation. But there are real limits to what the internet can provide in the way of professional advice. In the same way we can overreact by diagnosing ourselves via WebMD, it's not the best idea to craft an entire legal strategy from information gleaned from Google search results. In an estate dispute within a blended family, the Amateur Google Legal Expert will claim to other family members to have found the ultimate answer to their troubles, and thus any lawyer who doesn't go along with the plan is a fool.[1] While there are definitely foolish lawyers out there, we're confident that experience, training, and credibility in probate and trust litigation are worth their weight in gold. We don't readily embrace a legal strategy fully worked out by a nonprofessional armed with a mouse and three hours of Google time.

The 360-Degree Accuser

In blended-family estate disputes this character appears on the scene with regularity, pointing a finger of blame at everyone but themselves. Maybe it's a stepbrother or stepsister who seems to find everything wrong with every other member of the family, leveling all sorts of accusations, from estate theft to undue influence and even murder. Now, all those nefarious acts do occasionally take place in estate cases, but somehow the 360-Degree Accuser manages to fit most of the family into some outrageous scheme. The 360-Degree Accuser, meanwhile, is always totally innocent of any wrongdoing and would never be hiding something behind all their wild claims.

The Forgetter

This may be a stepparent or stepsibling who conveniently "forgets" the details of important trust and estate documents, or even where they were placed. The Forgetter might even hide the will, hoping that it will be flushed down the memory hole.[2] Often this will coincide with the Forgetter taking family heirlooms, jewelry, cash, and other estate property for themselves, contrary to the terms of the will or trust. If they're summoned for a deposition in trust or probate litigation, they'll likely suffer "memory loss" on important points in the case. All that the Forgetter has concealed, however, will ultimately be revealed in the discovery process of estate litigation.

The Substance Abuser

The Substance Abuser is a common character in estate fights involving blended families. Many times a family will have a "black sheep," and sometimes that child—or stepchild—will have a problem with substance abuse. Whether the issue is with alcohol, prescription drugs (a nationwide challenge), or illegal narcotics, addiction is a debilitating condition that can generate further bad-faith behavior by the Substance Abuser, including the conversion of estate funds and assets to fuel their drug habit. Entire family fortunes that took decades to build can be flushed down the drain by the Substance Abuser, but there are ways to set up preventive measures in estate plans, which I'll address in the next chapter.

The Talker

Our job is to help our clients and protect their interests. That means that we need the best possible accounting of all estate assets, and any documentation from reputable third parties should be chased down immediately. With a blended-family situation, however, things can get lost in the shuffle or even "forgotten" by bad actors looking to enrich themselves at others' expense (see "The Forgetter," above). That's where the Talker comes in. A good probate litigation attorney requires a clear view of all the funds and property in a trust or estate, but the Talker doesn't provide much help. The Talker will tell stories of hidden riches (big talk) or gossip about their family members or neighbors (small talk), yet when it comes to concrete estate matters, they have little of substance to offer that would protect their interests.

The Screamer

The Screamer is easy to recognize in an estate fight between stepchildren/half-children and stepparents—they raise the volume in the room all the way to 11, in the immortal words of Spinal Tap rocker Nigel Tufnel. While some people can understandably be frustrated by the outrageous behavior of an estate wrongdoer or the circumstances of the litigation process, the Screamer takes every opportunity to charge the atmosphere with unnecessary emotional tension and start a fight where there wasn't one to begin with. The Screamer is mostly about making noise, but without substantive facts, all the noise in the world won't prove their status as a rightful trust beneficiary or heir to an estate.

That ends my observations—however tongue-in-cheek—of some of the common characters involved in estate, probate, and trust litigation. Just remember, your good sense can make a world of difference in solving an estate dispute. With a good, experienced probate litigator on your side, you're already several steps ahead.

John F. Kennedy Was Right: Life Is Unfair

With so many different moving pieces in families, and with estate planning and wills always being imperfect, inequalities may be relatively common. More often than not, the family house gets sold because none of the siblings or stepsiblings can agree to allow one of the siblings to continue living there, or because one or more of the siblings just wants the cash. Or maybe Dad had a beautiful painting and two children both wanted it. Who gets the painting? The eldest, the favorite, or the one who grabs it first? Maybe Dad should have taken a King Solomon approach and given half of his priceless Picasso to each! We've seen cases where one stepsibling received a fraction less property than another stepsibling and spent thousands of dollars in legal fees to achieve what she believed was parity.

Such ridiculous situations are extremely common, and not always in cases where the dollar amounts are large. Unequal inheritance is always emotionally charged, and often brings with it decades of disputes, grievances, and perceived slights. In the end, we may all die, but fights over estate property will go on forever.

With that in mind, here are some suggestions for how to handle conflict in an unequal-inheritance dispute involving siblings, stepsiblings, and half-siblings:

1. **Try to leave emotions out of the equation.** I use the word "try" because I know how hard it can be to be completely cold and rational about an inheritance that was less than fair. Attorneys often get involved in these matters precisely because the parties involved are too close to the problem and can't be detached or unemotional enough to make the hard decisions.

2. **Decide how much "fair" is worth.** Can you put a dollar amount on the inequality in the inheritance? Did one sibling receive the house in Tahoe worth $3 million while the other got an apartment in San Ramon worth $1 million? Maybe when Dad drew up his will he was trying to be fair, and both properties had the same value. Maybe the house appreciated faster than the apartment, which led to a disparity. If there is truly a major difference, it might be worth trying to find a way to solve that imbalance. But when the disparity might be $10,000 or even $100,000, you have to decide whether the inevitable attorney's fees and court costs, not to mention fractured relationships, will be worth the fight.

3. **Before heading to court, consider using a mediator.** Maybe Dad or Mom was always the one to mediate and keep the peace. When they pass away, instead of "lawyering up" perhaps you should

consider hiring a mediator to try to work out a brokered peace. Unlike a court decision, the decision of a mediator isn't necessarily binding; both parties can agree that the decision isn't workable or fair, in which case you may still wind up in court. But at least trying the mediation approach first may solve many of the inequality issues, and a good mediator may find a way to not only divide up the estate equitably but also keep relationships from getting frayed.

4. **Remember that "fair" doesn't always mean equal.** There are cases where Dad or Mom wisely left more for one child because in his or her opinion one child needed more than the other. Sometimes the giver knows what fair is more than the receiver.

No Will, No Way? Not Necessarily

Consider the following scenario, which happens all the time: Uncle Buster tells you that you're going to inherit his house. You love your Uncle Buster, and you want him to live to ripe old age, but you know in your heart that when Uncle Buster dies, you will inherit his house because it's what he wants. Uncle Buster also lets a few other relatives and neighbors know that he was eventually going to give you the house.

Sadly, Uncle Buster dies.

Aunt Thelma, Buster's long-lost sister, shows up at the funeral and announces that she's in charge of Buster's estate. You're initially too shy to ask her about Buster's will, but you're concerned. Within days, Thelma is cleaning out the house and getting all of its contents ready for a Saturday garage sale.

You stop by the sale and get up the nerve to talk to your aunt. "Aunt Thelma, Uncle Buster told me that I was going to inherit his house. Do you have his will?"

"No such thing," Thelma responds. "It's none of your business, and you should be ashamed of yourself." She says that Buster didn't have a will anyway.

You call your attorney to see what legal right you have to the home. Well, in a word: none.

Every state, and the District of Columbia, has intestacy laws establishing who gets property after the death of a loved one who dies without a will. In this case, Uncle Buster dies without a spouse, without issue (i.e., without children and grandchildren), and his only survivor is his estranged sister, Thelma.

So, who gets the house? Thelma!

This might seem unfair (particularly if you suspect that Thelma destroyed his will). But probate rules throughout the United States, enacted to ensure that property is distributed according to a deceased person's wishes, require that wills be in writing.

Without a will, the decedent is said to be "intestate," and the state's probate rules define who takes a decedent's property. This is, surprisingly, a situation that happens often—even to the rich and famous. Amy Winehouse, Sonny Bono, and Abraham Lincoln all died without wills.[1] When the singer-songwriter Prince died in April 2016, he left behind a fortune of more than $200 million— and no will. More than forty-five "relatives" came forward to claim part of Prince's estate, including at least one prison inmate who maintained he was an illegitimate and long-lost son (sorry, no DNA match). In the end, Prince's sister and five half-siblings were ruled the rightful heirs, which may not have been what Prince wanted had he thought to create a will.[2]

What If the Will Is Wrong?

In 2015, the California Supreme Court issued a new ruling that changes certain aspects of probate and estate law. By a 7–0 unanimous decision, the court ruled that errors in a testator's will can be remedied according to evidence of the deceased individual's intentions.[3]

In the case that prompted the decision, a widower left behind a multimillion-dollar estate without a clear designation of who would inherit the fortune. Irving Duke, a Los Angeles County resident who died in 2007, passed away with a will that was composed in 1984, when he was still married. In the event he and his wife died at the same time, Duke planned for his property and funds to be entrusted to two charities. (He left $1 to his brother and disinherited everyone else.)

Life, as we know, doesn't always go according to our plan. Duke's wife ended up dying in 2002, and he never changed his will before he himself died five years later. A judge at the county superior court level, as well an appeals court, said that absent any specification within the will, Duke's assets would be distributed to his closest living relatives, his two nephews.

Once the Duke case made it to the California Supreme Court, however, a new precedent for interpreting contested wills was set. Chief Justice Tani Cantil-Sakauye stated that the inability to revise a faulty or incomplete will to reflect a testator's original intent could "unjustly enrich those who would inherit as a result of a mistake."[4] With her decision, Justice Cantil-Sakauye effectively reversed a 1965 ruling upholding the position that a will's written provisions were binding, no matter the testator's intent.

So what does the court's new ruling on wills mean for potential estate disputes in California? Although the decision seems to upend hundreds of years of judicial precedent (going back to the times of Henry VIII, no less), it's important to consider that wills remain the basic tool of estate law in California. Now, however, if a will document contains errors or omissions, we can right the wrong with *evidence* of the deceased's *intent*. And that's a positive step for protecting intended beneficiaries in the event of litigation. Proving someone's intent once they are dead is still a very big obstacle, but at least there is a path that attorneys and heirs can take to address egregious errors.

Wills and Undue Influence

The roots of twenty-first century inheritance laws run deep into the cradle of Western civilization. The ancient Greek Athenian leader Solon made great efforts to devise a law code that ultimately became one of the foundations of democracy and helped establish rules for a civilized society. It's probably not surprising, then, that part of the code addressed inheritance rights. Before the code, an Athenian could not make a will. At death, the wealth and assets of the decedent simply belonged to his family.

Solon changed this. An Athenian, if he had no children, could by will distribute at death his wealth and assets to whomever he pleased. In Plutarch's epic work *Lives of the Noble Grecians and Romans*, he argued that this change allowed the decedent to decide "that he esteemed friendship a stronger tie than kindred, affection than necessity; and made every man's estate truly his own."[5]

Solon also advanced the idea that wealth and asset transfers that resulted from undue influence could be negated or set aside. While Solon may not have used the term "undue influence," his description of the actions that could negate a will are colorful and give us a pretty good idea of what he was talking about.

Plutarch wrote that Solon

> allowed not all sorts of legacies, but those only which were not extorted by the frenzy of a disease, charms, imprisonment, force, or the persuasion of a wife; with good reason thinking that being seduced into wrong was as bad as being forced, and that between deceit and necessity, flattery and compulsion, there was little difference, since both may equally suspend the exercise of reason.[6]

Fast forward (well, not that far forward) to early-seventeenth-century England. Sir Francis Bacon is the judge in a court case with wide-ranging repercussions. In the suit, Bacon learns of the following facts:

- A married woman named Anne Death "worked on [the] simplicity and weakness" of George Lydiatt, an eighty-year-old man, "by her dalliance and pretence of love . . . and by sundry adulterous courses with him."

- Lydiatt executed a will and deed giving her his entire estate, which included property and land with a value "of upwards of £3,000," disinheriting his next-of-kin, his niece.

- Having secured Lydiatt's full inheritance, Death "used him in a most cruel manner reviling him and causing him to be whipped and suffered him to be loathsome and uncleanly in bed."

- The man's niece and her husband filed suit against the woman.

Sir Francis Bacon ruled that the deed and will were void, and that the woman should receive "exemplary punishment." This case set our modern precedent for a claim of "undue influence."[7]

California's twenty-first-century legal definition of undue influence may lack the flair of Solon (through Plutarch) and Bacon, but it gets the point across:

> 'Undue influence' means excessive persuasion that causes another person to act or refrain from acting by overcoming that person's free will and results in inequity.
>
> In determining whether a result was produced by undue influence, all of the following shall be considered:
>
> 1. The vulnerability of the victim. . . .
> 2. The influencer's authority. . . .
> 3. The actions or tactics used by the influencer. . . .
> 4. The equity of the result. . . .[8]

In my daily life as a trust, estate, and elder financial abuse litigator, those are the four factors I constantly refer to when looking at a will and deciding whether undue influence may have played a role in its creation.

Trying to Hide the Will?
We'll See about That.

One common tactic employed by perpetrators of fraud in estate and probate cases is to hide documents. If key estate documents like a will or trust suddenly "disappear," the wrongdoer believes, the rights of lawful beneficiaries will also supposedly be canceled out. For an example of this game of estate hide-and-seek, let's look at a hypothetical story based on real circumstances we come across in everyday estate law here in California:

Three adult children learn of the death of their father, Bob, from cancer. The news of Bob's passing comes as no surprise, since he had been battling it for several years. In the year before his death, Bob outlined how to divide his property and assets among his children in a living trust. After Bob dies, however, the children don't receive what was promised them according to estate documents. Not only that, but Bob's widow Betty, their stepmother, begins claiming the children's rightly inherited property, from vehicles and heirlooms to valuable real estate, as her own.

When Bob's kids try to talk to their stepmother about properly distributing the estate assets, she denies Bob's original wishes for his family. The children then point to Bob's will, which specifically delineates the division of the estate among them. That's when Betty goes so far as to hide Bob's will, lying that she doesn't know where it went and that it must have gotten "lost" in the shuffle after his passing. Betty thinks she's in the clear, that she can now enjoy Bob's estate for herself without having to fulfill her late husband's actual intentions.

What Betty doesn't realize is that the law will ensure she's caught in her own lie. California State Probate Code Sections 8870–8873 allow for parties in an estate dispute to be summoned to court and be examined under oath. Should they attempt to evade this summons, their actions can be equated to contempt of court, with all the consequences that entails.[9] If wrongdoers like Betty have stolen, concealed, or sold estate property that wasn't rightfully theirs, they can be prosecuted.

As this scenario shows, a missing will can create problems, but those problems aren't necessarily insurmountable.

How to Get a Lost Will Admitted to Probate Court

California probate lawyers and estate litigators know that documents are easily lost. Even the National Archives has an extensive list of missing items.[10] Is it any wonder, then, that we ordinary people also lose documents? When it comes to wills and trusts, lost documents can shatter the expectations set by a family's estate planning. A family's wealth transfer expectations, often discussed within a family or collectively assumed by a family while parents are alive, are sometimes challenged by the crafty finagling of an outside bad actor (or family member). Some documents may mysteriously go missing, while new documents may sometimes mysteriously appear. The ingenuity of people seeking to push their own agendas knows few bounds.

Many times I have heard suspicions that a family member destroyed a will to enhance their inheritance. We find remedies to deal with such wrongdoing, but generally, the legal solutions are neither immediate nor inexpensive. Sometimes the simple embarrassment or humiliation that comes from being exposed as a wrongdoer will prompt the "rediscovery" of a will or trust initially said to be lost.

Families in grief—or that are expecting an inheritance—can be unpredictable. At times a lone member of the family can act as a one-person wrecking crew of family unity. That said, and without identifying all the ways that we use to "smoke out" a lost will or trust,[11] know that there *are* some probate legal procedures addressing the probate of a lost will that may be used when important documents are "lost" or destroyed.

Early questions arise at the start of a probate matter as to the absence of a will, among them:

- What can we do if the will has been lost for years?

- Do we need to have witnesses that know the contents of the will?

- What else do we need to know to get a lost will admitted to probate?

- May a draft of a will be an acceptable substitute?

Let's start with the law. California Probate Code Section 6124 provides:

> If the testator's will was last in the testator's possession, the testator was competent until death, and neither the will nor a duplicate original of the will can be found after the testator's death, it is presumed that the testator destroyed the will with intent to revoke it. This presumption is a presumption affecting the burden of producing evidence.[12]

In other words, assuming there's no copy of the will and no evidence to overcome this presumption, the decedent's assets (except those excluded from probate) will probably pass intestate, which means that the estate is handled according to California statute.

Sometimes, though, there *is* evidence that the will was not destroyed. For example, the decedent may have shared a copy of the will and asked his relative to keep it in a safe place. Such a copy—again, depending on the evidence—may be valid and admitted to probate.

In California, the petition for probate of a lost or destroyed will must "include a written statement of the testamentary words or their substance. If the will is proved, the provisions of the will shall be set forth in the order admitting the will to probate."[13] Stated more simply, if there was a will but it can't be found, all is not necessarily lost. If the terms of the will—the testator's intentions—can be proven by testimony, there is a possibility that a court might find the terms persuasive and that they "prove" the will. Nevertheless, this is more than a challenging task, not easily accomplished, and will likely meet the skepticism of an overburdened probate judge.

Challenging Wills and Trusts

In popular culture, a boogeyman is a mythical creature that frightens children into good behavior, or just plain frightens children. A boogeyman's description relies upon a child's own imagination. I can still recall that around my kindergarten years my imagined boogeyman was a gorilla who hid alternately in my closet, under the bed, or in the dining room.

As children, we might have been told that if we didn't behave, the boogeyman would get us. While we mature we put the fears of the mythical boogeyman behind us. That said, there are parts of our culture and lives that retain a boogeyman-like aura. No-contest clauses in California wills and trusts have that characteristic. They are designed to deter trust or will challenges by enforcing a statutory disinheritance penalty on estate challengers. In other words, "If you challenge this will or trust you'll lose everything—or maybe you'll get $1." The boogeyman is at work. No one wants to trigger an automatic penalty that they believe will cause them to lose everything, so such clauses can be highly effective. The no-contest clause has scared off many greedy heirs who might want to mount a challenge but aren't willing to gamble on a win-lose coin toss.

Now, let's talk about what this boogeyman should **not** be protecting:

- a drug-addled son who is unduly influencing his vulnerable mother to change her trust and leave everything to him.

- a caretaker controlling the necessities of life of an elderly adult who transports the elder to an attorney of the caretaker's choosing and while there revises the will to leave the elder's house to the caretaker and any Goodwill bags to the elder's four children.

- a long-out-of-work daughter living with her Alzheimer's-stricken mother who convinces her mother to change her trust to exclude her three siblings from receiving anything.

My law firm challenges wills and trusts with great regularity. And, in fact, most of the wills or trusts we challenge have "no-contest" clauses written into them. So what? While I won't say that we cut through all of them like a hot knife through butter, I will say that we make certain that our client's challenges meet the probable cause standard of California's probate code, which can often override a no-contest clause. The statute says that "probable cause exists if, at the time of filing a contest, the facts known to the contestant would cause a reasonable person to believe that there is a reasonable likelihood that the requested relief will be granted after an opportunity for further investigation or discovery."[14]

The important qualifiers to no-contest clauses include the recognition that probable cause exists if a reasonable person thinks there is a reasonable likelihood of success after an opportunity for further investigation or discovery. In estate litigation, most facts are not known at the initiation of a will or trust contest. There are often telltale signs of financial elder abuse or undue influence that still require follow-ups. Litigation is often the follow-up.

I have seen too many cases where a wrongdoer plays the no-contest clause as a "get out of jail free" card. I just won't buy it. When there is estate wrongdoing, I move forward with every expectation that the relief that we seek will be granted after there has been an opportunity for further investigation or discovery.

Estate wrongdoers should take little comfort when asserting the no-contest boogeyman against abused trust beneficiaries and estate heirs. If someone invokes the boogeyman against you by asserting that a will is "ironclad" and has a "no-contest clause," you don't have to let that deter you. You will, however, need to find an attorney who is not afraid to stand up for clients and isn't afraid of the boogeyman. That said, no-contest clause are enforced in varied ways in our country's different states. Local counsel will need to make a reasoned analysis of whether the identified no-contest clause is a boogeyman or an easily enforced forfeiture clause against a will or trust challenger.

A Will Is Still the Foundation of Any Estate Plan

Most people understand the purpose of a will and the importance of having one in place, yet statistics show that an astonishingly high percentage of Americans have not drafted one. A 2016 Gallup poll found that almost half of US residents between the ages of fifty and sixty-four do not have a will.[15]

The reasons people give for not having one range from "I haven't gotten around to making one" (57 percent) to "I don't want to think about death" (14 percent). Somewhere in between those two groups are people without wills who simply aren't sure where to turn for assistance creating one.

If you have a will in place, but it has not been reviewed by a lawyer for five or more years, it is time to do so. Life changes—divorce, remarriage, the death of a spouse, etc.—require regularly reviewing a will to ensure that it still accomplishes your objectives.

Even though at best it is far from a perfect document, a will is the foundation of a comprehensive estate plan that protects your loved ones and ensures that your assets are distributed according to your wishes when you die. The simple truth is, if there are people in your life whom you love, then you need a will. Wills really do what they are supposed to do most of the time.

You should also consider creating a durable power of attorney so someone can make financial decisions on your behalf in case you become incapacitated, and advance health care directives for the same reason. Many individuals are also well served by trusts, which can help your estate avoid probate, minimize taxes, provide accountability, and accomplish many other objectives.

In sum, here are a few words of advice to those Uncle Busters who like to express their wishes but don't have it in writing: "If wishes were fishes we'd all swim in riches."

Learn from Uncle Buster's sad story:

- Get your wishes into a will, a trust, or other writing that secures your wishes.

- If you have an attorney, make sure they have a copy of your will. That way, if an Aunt Thelma shows up and says there is no will, you'll have a backup.

If you're Uncle Buster and you want your niece to inherit your house, make sure she also has a copy of your will!

Safes and Safe Deposit Boxes

Very little has been written about safes and safe deposit boxes in estates, which surprises me because so many of my cases involve families that use them. Banks generally only send one invoice per year for a safe deposit box, and the charge is usually debited directly from the holder's checking account. If you weren't looking for it, you could easily miss that $79 annual charge.

An unexpectedly large number of people open safe deposit boxes, leave them alone for several years, and then forget the box ever existed. According to the *Sacramento Bee*, in 2017 the California State Controller's Office had the contents of more than 138,000 safe deposit boxes under its control, including more than 75,000 US savings bonds; the combined value of the bonds was more than $30 million.[1] Sometimes banks move, and sometimes box holders move, but the usual way boxes get forgotten is when someone dies.

While safe deposit boxes can, and usually do, serve a useful purpose of safeguarding valuables, you should know that they aren't 100 percent safe. Take, for example, the following case, reported in a 2007 *Consumer Reports* blog post. The day after her sister died, a woman visited a Bank of America safe deposit vault in Manhattan to close out her sister's accounts—only to discover that her "sister" had supposedly been there earlier that day! Far from being a miracle, it was instead a con job. According to the blog post, a "friend" of the woman's sister had taken control of her assets, and the day after she died this friend went to the bank, showed the bank the sister's ID, forged her signature on the box register, and proceeded to walk away with an estimated $75,000 in cash plus jewelry. The bank branch manager refused to cooperate with a subsequent investigation, perhaps believing that cooperation would lead to liability.[2] Such cases are probably rare, but they do illustrate an important point, namely that you can't always count on banks to help in estate matters involving safe deposit boxes.

Safe deposit boxes add a mix of mystery and distrust to disputed estates. Their secrecy enfolds the basic questions that heirs and beneficiaries of disputed estates strive to answer—questions beginning with "who," "what," "where," "when," and "how."[3] The "why" for estate wrongdoing might combine a number of motives, but it doesn't take crack investigative skills to spot the primary one—financial gain.

Unfortunately—and shockingly to many people who find out the hard way—the contents of most safe deposit boxes are not insured. A $10,000 deposit at a bank usually carries FDIC insurance, but if you put $10,000 in a safe deposit box at the same bank and someone in your family loots the box, your options will be limited. You would need to prove that the bank was negligent to have a case, although it will probably only occur to most people to buy such insurance after a worst-case scenario has already happened.[4]

Estates often have a mix of assets, and administering them without the assistance of experienced and skilled counsel can be complicated and fraught. Anxiety fueled by grief is an inevitable part of the inventorying process of a decedent's property. A family member is tasked by practicality, family consensus, or an estate document to gather a decedent's assets. Some assets are apparent—a house, documented bank accounts and securities, onsite personal property. Other assets are more opaque, such as those physically separated in a financial institution's safe deposit box or inside a house or office safe. All the while, there is uncertainty and stress.

Safe Deposit Law

Safe deposit boxes have long been regulated in California. Even regulated, however, their existence still presents opportunities for mischief from wrongdoers. California Probate Code Section 331 limits access to a decedent's safe deposit box. The limitations apply only to a box held by a decedent alone or a decedent and others who are also deceased. The code does not affect the rights of a living co-holder.[5]

If the box is in the decedent's name alone, section 331 allows for any person who has a key to the box to gain access before a personal estate representative is appointed to settle the estate. Access is granted for the limited purpose of establishing an inventory, making a photocopy of all wills and trusts in the box, and securing instructions for the disposition of the decedent's remains. If a will is found, it must be mailed or delivered to the clerk of the superior court. A copy of the will is required to be provided to the named executor or beneficiaries.

If there is no key to the decedent's safe deposit box, the person seeking access must obtain letters testamentary from the superior court to gain access to the box.

If we apply the classic journalists' questions—the five Ws and an H—to a decedent's safe deposit box, the following inquiries come up: Who had access to the box before the decedent's death? Who had access to it after the death? What was in the box before the death? After the death? Where was the box located? Were there other accounts with the financial institution at the same location? When was the box leased from the financial institution? When was the box accessed? Why did the decedent lease the box? Why did the decedent tell (or not tell) others about the box? How did anyone other than the decedent gain access to the box?

Safe deposit boxes become part of estate and trust litigation in a variety of ways. In cases where the decedent was the sole holder of the box, access visits shortly before their death may raise issues of undue influence—particularly if there are dramatic changes in estate plans around the same time as the visits.

What happens when a family member or even the executor or trustee of an estate is suspected of having taken something of value out of a decedent's safe deposit box? Maybe a trustee took his aunt's collection of gold coins from a safe deposit box and denied the existence of the collection when challenged by the trust's beneficiaries.

Wrongdoers are not always logical. Discovery of their wrongdoing is often bewildering to reasonable people with an established set of cherished values. When estate wrongdoing is discovered, disbelief on the part of the victim is a common reaction, followed by anger.

My firm is usually hired to do estate or trust litigation at the abused beneficiary's anger stage. Our clients often express to us that they have to overcome their deep sense of disbelief before hiring a probate or trust litigation attorney. We understand; we've protected many clients from sociopaths who prey on the unsuspecting. We are hired to hold wrongdoers accountable and to collect what they wrongfully took from an heir or beneficiary. This is not always an easy task. Wrongdoers operate in the shadows, and once discovered they might vigorously fight efforts to bring them to justice and accountability. Sociopaths have no shame or sense of responsibility, and they'll lie right up to the end if it's convenient for them.

What are the steps rightful heirs should take when they believe that someone has wrongfully obtained property from a safe or safe deposit box? Here are five to consider. (As you may notice, many of them overlap quite a bit with the steps you should take if you are cut out of a will or trust, as discussed in Chapter 1.)

1) Assess Damages

- As I ask all of my clients and prospective clients, "How much is really at stake?" The grief, anger, and sense of betrayal that can accompany an estate dispute can blind the parties to the particulars of the damages. No matter how much outrage the loss of Uncle Louie's horse blanket engenders, it is still only a horse blanket and probably not worth more than a few dollars.

- What was the estate worth? Sometimes the answer comes easily—"There was a $50,000 bank account." However, it's not always so easy:

"Well, there's the duplex in Arcata, the ranch in Sonoma, the house in East Sacramento, the bank account at Wells Fargo, the IRA at Golden One, and the stock portfolio at Schwab. And don't forget the life insurance policies, the bonds in the Tahoe safe deposit box, and the timeshares in Cuernavaca." You get the idea; this might take some time.

- In any event, there are lots of ways to prove damages and lots of ways to be damaged. A skilled litigation counsel will examine and develop these factors and provide much-needed perspective. You may be irate that some precious family heirloom was taken by someone who had no right to it, but the cost of getting that object back may not be worth the struggle, both in terms of dollars and emotional energy. It's often easier for someone like an attorney, who is not emotionally invested in the dispute, to help you make that call.

2) Remember that Time Is of the Essence

- Settlements to get property back are usually struck after a lawsuit—not before. That said, experienced counsel on opposites sides of a dispute might explore settlement early, as they know the costs and burdens of litigation.

- The law does not reward those who delay seeking their rights. There are several very restrictive time limits for filing will and trust litigation matters. If you believe that your case may be disputed, seek counsel. It's that simple.

3) Do Your Homework

- With every case I take, I ask clients to help me prepare a timeline of the facts of the case. The events and actions in a client's story can be a compelling way to highlight exploitation. Chronology is also important to establish a valid claim under a particular statute of limitations.

- We also need to know what the current status of the case is. Did the executor sell the assets and move to Ecuador? Is he still in town and enjoying his new Cadillac?

- In certain extreme cases, it may be necessary to hire a private investigator to track down either people or property.

- Is there a probate proceeding pending in the local probate court? Is a trust administration pending? Actions concerning court-supervised trusts may also be pending in the local probate court.

4) Make a Plan

- Remember the adage "He who fails to plan, plans to fail." It's just as true when it comes to trusts and estates.

- Hire an experienced estate litigation lawyer to assist you.

- Remember that an internet search does not make you an expert. The probate litigator probably understands quite a lot more than you do after a four-hour Google search.

- Identify the steps in your plan.

- Figure out how the costs of estate litigation are going to be paid. Hourly? By contingency fee? A combination of a reduced hourly rate with a contingency fee?

5) Decide If You Want a Jury Trial

- There are special rules concerning the availability of jury trials in probate and estate matters.

- We often file estate-related matters in the California Superior Court for civil cases because we like to reserve the right to a jury trial. That said, there are some matters that by law belong and stay in the probate division of the superior court, where cases are tried by a judge and not a jury. Weighing the costs and benefits of a jury trial will almost always factor into the decision of whether to pursue someone who has wrongfully obtained a decedent's property.

As always, when in doubt about what to do when wrongdoing is suspected, you should consult with a qualified and experienced attorney who is conversant in the laws of personal property in trusts and estates. Every case has unique nuances, and the facts of each determine the appropriate course of action.

Fraud and Fraud Detection

S everal times per month, someone calls me to report that they suspect that their late mother/aunt/cousin has been defrauded, and they need to know if there is anything they can do about it. In most cases, they believe that a trusted advisor, fiduciary, or other professional has taken advantage of their elderly relative who recently died. Other times, a relative or a friend of the deceased is suspected of fraud. Do they have a case? Can justice be served? Is the money or property truly gone?

I tell them that it is critically important to first establish the facts and then build a very strong timeline of events that lets us know when the first injury occurred and if the fraud could have been prevented. Who allegedly committed the fraud? How was the fraud committed? When did the fraud occur? Unless there are solid facts to back up assertions, there will probably be no case to pursue. To win justice, you will need more than just a hunch.

Here is a very typical fact pattern and timeline for someone I'll call Sarah:

- Sarah is an eighty-three-year-old widow living alone in Santa Monica.

- Sarah has a net worth of $900,000, excluding her personal residence. Sarah's properties are titled in the name of the Sarah Revocable Trust, which was established by her late husband.

- Sarah is the customer of registered representative Bubba and has $500,000 invested with the brokerage firm where Bubba works, ABC.

- Bubba is registered with FINRA (the Financial Industry Regulatory Authority) through ABC.

- In 2015, Sarah begins experiencing significant cognitive decline associated with Alzheimer's disease. She subsequently suffers from dementia and memory loss.

- In late 2015, Bubba unduly influences Sarah to change her trust, naming him as the trustee and beneficiary of the trust.

- Bubba neither informs ABC of his actions nor secures ABC's consent to his activity with a firm customer.

- Sarah dies in July 2016.

- Bubba takes control of the trust assets and prepares to distribute the assets to himself as the sole beneficiary of the trust.

- Sarah's heirs hire a law firm to nullify Sarah's last trust amendment that names Bubba as the sole beneficiary.

- ABC and Bubba are notified of the pending actions.

You might think that such an event could not happen easily. After all, don't securities firms have ways to detect such fraud? A registered representative must surely know that they will be caught, right? Unfortunately, in most cases, people like our fictional Bubba do get away with it. Why? Because people like Bubba typically choose their victims carefully. Remember, his position allows him to know a lot about his customers. In fact, it's part of his job to know intimate details about them.

Sarah is a typical victim: She lives alone and does not have any close relatives. She has no immediate heirs. She is beginning to have significant cognitive decline. (Bubba knows this because she sounds confused or incoherent over the phone.) He also knows that her estate will probably end up being transferred to the state upon her death, so he believes that taking her assets after she dies would be a "victimless crime." If no one is looking, and if no one seems to care, people like Bubba will seize customer assets that are easy to get and ripe for the taking.

It's not just unscrupulous brokers that perpetrate fraud on the elderly. Even attorneys, who are sworn to uphold the law, can turn out to be bad actors. Consider the matter of Connecticut attorney Peter Clark. In 2015, Clark, who was fifty-seven, made a plea bargain with the US attorney on charges of mail fraud. He had diverted a hefty $1.8 million from his deceased client's fortune, money which he then proceeded to use for his own purposes.

When Miriam Strong of Oxford, Connecticut, died in 2010, Clark was one of two lawyers appointed as executor of her estate. Before her death, Strong had wanted her substantial $4.3 million estate to be put to good use in the surrounding community; among designated beneficiaries she named schools, churches, and charities, even stating her intention to institute a scholarship for local students. But instead, Clark committed a profound violation of trust and stole over a third of Strong's estate funds for himself.

While Clark was partnered with another lawyer to act as the estate executor and supervise the distribution of money to beneficiaries, he used financial sleight-of-hand to funnel the money into his own pockets. After setting up a duplicate account for the estate without the knowledge of the other attorney, he began siphoning off funds for his own interests. To cover his tracks, he provided the probate court and beneficiaries with false accounting reports that concealed the fraud.

How was he found out? Some of the intended recipients of the late Strong's donations noticed that they weren't getting what they were originally promised. His fellow attorney also noticed something was amiss and found out from bank employees about the existence of Clark's dummy account. The FBI came on the scene, and Clark decided to plead out.[1]

Elder financial abuse and fraud are grave threats to the economy as well as the emotional and even physical well-being of our elderly loved ones. Whether it's an upscale neighborhood in Los Angeles, a hillside estate in Alameda County, or a multigenerational farm outside of Sacramento, nowhere are families immune from this form of exploitation. Called "the crime of the twenty-first century" by the American Bar Association,[2] elder financial abuse can range from unethical sales tactics and a variety of fraud schemes perpetrated by strangers to misappropriation of a senior's funds and assets, often by a family member. Other potential perpetrators can include caretakers, financial professionals, attorneys, or con artists posing as a "new friend."

Many times, elder financial abuse runs hand-in-hand with isolation, cognitive impairment on the part of the victim, undue influence, and neglect. Cases like contractor fraud, insurance fraud, investment fraud, and real estate fraud, as well as telemarketing scams, are all too frequently perpetrated against our elderly neighbors and loved ones. Senior citizens are also vulnerable to wrongdoing by their very own relatives; dishearteningly, this is actually the most common form of elder financial abuse. Abusers within a family will take advantage of their position to hijack their elders' bank accounts and steal their funds and property. Other times perpetrators of elder financial abuse will also misuse the power of attorney to defraud elderly victims, not to mention wield undue influence to unlawfully change estate documents like wills and trusts.

Litigation

My firm regularly represents victims of elder financial abuse and their families in litigation to protect their interests and hold bad actors accountable. Through my years of experience, I have seen it all. The good news is that over the past few years there's been a sea change in the way elder financial abuse is treated in California probate law. Now, in addition to criminal sanctions by authorities, victims and their families can bring legal action in civil courts. The Elder Abuse and Dependent Adult Civil Protection Act provides a means of recovery for those whose interests as estate heirs or trust beneficiaries have been violated. That means if a judge or jury see a preponderance of evidence that a perpetrator wrongfully took the property of a victim/decedent, they can be held accountable for the damage they caused as well as attorney's fees.[3]

Litigation in civil court means that a jury of your peers can hear your story, witness firsthand the tragic results of elder financial abuse, and punish the wrongdoer while making recovery possible. California's introduction of jury trials for financial exploitation of the elderly is proving to be a game-changer in protecting our communities' most vulnerable members against financial predators.

If you or a family member suspect fraud, there are some practical considerations you should make before you decide to proceed. One common challenge is whether family members can civilly prosecute these claims while the elder is alive. A problem often arises when the elder has not been determined to be incompetent even though family members may think that the elder obviously is.

Here are some considerations that should be addressed by you and your attorney before litigation:

- An elder is presumed to be competent until medical experts prove incapacity.

- An elder may change the beneficiaries of their trust while competent.

- The beneficiaries of a trust lack standing while the elder is alive and competent to change the terms of the trust.

- An effort by trust beneficiaries to have the elder deemed incompetent while the elder is alive may blow back on the challengers and cause them to be completely excluded from the trust.

- If the elder has not been deemed to be incompetent, the only people with standing to challenge a transfer are a guardian ad litem, appointed by the court, a holder of a power of attorney, or a guardian/conservator.

Attorney's fees are sometimes also an impediment to the prosecution of these cases. Elders who have been cheated out of their assets will not have the resources to pay hourly fees to attorneys to civilly prosecute their claims. Attorneys willing to take these cases on a contingency fee basis can help to move these cases along.

Because of attorney-client privilege and clients' rights to confidentiality and privacy, I cannot cite my own cases, but I can say that I have helped many elders who have transferred or were in the process of transferring their houses or other property to wrongdoers who defrauded or unduly influenced them. My firm has stopped transfers and gotten transfers reversed. We have also helped elders terminate powers of attorney that were being misused by the holders of the power; such misuse has included theft and property transfers. We have helped elders or their families put temporary holds on the disbursement of funds or securities from financial institutions. Indeed, we have conducted several trials and multiple mediations that resulted in the return of assets that were wrongfully transferred.

Even when it may appear too late to do anything, such is not always the case. Of course, the sooner elder financial abuse or fraud is detected, the better the chance for recovery of estate and trust assets on behalf of the victims.

Evidence of Elder Financial Abuse

What are the typical signs or red flags to look out for? According to the guidelines of the National Adult Protective Services Association, the following factors should be watched closely to avoid a potential personal tragedy and financial disaster:

- **Liabilities and unpaid bills:** What if an elderly loved one should have the means to pay the bills every month, but somehow their utilities get shut off? There might be more in play than just a senior's faulty memory—a swindler may have made off with money from the elder's accounts, leaving the victim high and dry.

- **Surrender of oversight:** Very often we see cases where a "new friend," neighbor, or opportunistic relative appears on the scene to offer their "help" in managing the elder's financial accounts. At times they even succeed in gaining power of attorney. This effective forfeiture of oversight should be looked into closely, as it may indicate other suspicious activities.

- **Suspicious withdrawals:** Like any good investigator will tell you, follow the money. When financial accounts begin registering unexplained withdrawals or checks made out to "cash," it's time for you to speak with bank employees and get further details on who's making these transactions.

- **Vanishing assets:** Another telltale sign of elder financial abuse is that valuables begin to disappear.

Suddenly an elder's jewelry, cash, or financial documents (like stock certificates) vanish, and the perpetrator takes to living lavishly with new purchases of fancy attire, vehicles, property, etc.

- **Changed estate documents:** Wrongdoers who commit elder financial abuse will often seek to cover their predatory behavior with a stamp of legitimacy. Exercising undue influence on the elderly victim, they'll shop around for any lawyer who will agree to change a will or trust document in their favor. Ask your elderly loved one about any such changes. If you are faced with such a situation, it may be time to consult an experienced trust litigation attorney.

- **Creditors come knocking:** Is the elder encountering financial trouble where there should be none? Find out the explanation for property liens or foreclosure warnings. The reason behind a creditor's claims may be more than just a mistake—your elderly family member might have been financially exploited by an abuser who cleaned out their accounts.

Protective Measures Against Elder Financial Abuse

What are some initial steps you can take to stop elder financial abuse? Several measures are available to family members, lawyers, financial professionals, and medical caregivers. Along with basic awareness, coordination and ongoing communication between parties translate to increased protection. Here are some basic actions you can take to keep elderly loved ones safe from exploitation:

- **Financial oversight:** A family member and a financial professional at the elder's local bank or advisory firm should establish a system of oversight over an elder's accounts. In addition to setting up automatic bill payment, keep a sharp eye on any excessive withdrawals or irregular transfers. Consider joint accounts with the elder, and look into the possibility of a limited credit card for an elder susceptible to financial exploitation.

- **Revocable trusts:** With a revocable trust in place, a trustee has access to a trust account without the status of legal ownership. Stopping irresponsible or just plain bad trustees from squandering assets translates to built-in and effective safeguards.

- **Communication:** The human element is vital in preventing elder financial abuse, and that means maintaining effective lines of communication between all interested parties, whether they be the elder's attorney, investment advisor, and/or medical caregiver. Just as importantly, a loving relationship with an elderly family member makes all the difference in shielding them from harm. If a senior is lonely, they'll be more vulnerable to fraud or unethical sales pitches. Just visiting an elder regularly, talking to them and showing them you care, is an enormous boost in keeping them safe.

- **No-contact lists:** "Boiler room" telemarketers and deceptive mailers target elders who suffer from cognitive impairment. One way to block most, if not all, of these unwelcome solicitors is to contact the FTC's Do Not Call Registry, Nomorobo, and the Direct Marketing Association. Speak with your elderly loved one about the harmful nature of these calls and flyers to help them spot when they're being scammed.

Cons and Caretakers

It seems so simple: "Honor thy father and thy mother." This commandment, deeply embedded in our Judeo-Christian heritage, is a part of the fabric of our daily lives. This fabric draws little notice—that is, until an incident happens or circumstance arises and unnerves us.

Millions of Americans are unnerved by the scourges of dementia and Alzheimer's, both patients and their family members. Family members can be torn in different ways, but they all create uncertainty as to whether action or inaction is called for when it comes to protecting a parent.[1]

Children of Alzheimer's patients are challenged in so many aspects. Here is one example showcasing what they may face:

Dad is retired. Mom died five years ago. Dad owns his own home in Brentwood, an expensive neighborhood in Los Angeles. He has a secure income in retirement and some liquid investments. Dad's three children live nearby—a daughter in Santa Monica, another daughter in Irvine, and a son in San Clemente.

The siblings get along well, call each other often, and share updates about their father. The shared updates include information that Dad is becoming more secretive, less willing to talk about his finances, and increasingly guarded on the phone.

Dad's housekeeper is a constant presence with him. The siblings learn that Dad has given her at least $75,000 over the last two years. The children call me. They tell me the story. They wonder what they can do.

I do some quick fact-gathering. Does Dad have a trust? Who is the trustee? Are any of the children on Dad's accounts? If not, who, if anyone else, is on the accounts? Has Dad been diagnosed with any disease?

I ask them to describe Dad's memory and his cognitive functioning, his ability to carry on in everyday life. Have the three siblings met with Dad and discussed their concerns? Will Dad give one or more of the siblings a power of attorney to assist him with his finances? If not, is there an alternative to a conservatorship of his estate to protect him? Are there other methods that might protect Dad against elder financial abuse?

There are, but as the old saying goes, "It's complicated." In the meantime, an unsettling ambivalence takes over the children. If we move to protect Dad, they wonder, will he be mad at us? Freeze us out of his life? Write us out of the will? Become so separated from us that protecting him will become only harder?

If we don't move to protect him, will he give everything to the housekeeper? Lose what cognitive ability that he has left? Become oblivious to those around him?

These are tough questions, questions that should be asked. Better to consider them than ignore the obvious. In the end, children who want to honor their father and their mother might find doing so requires difficult choices. At what point do we intervene and at what point do we step back? It's not always clear.

The Mickey Rooney Case

Do you remember Mickey Rooney, the lovable veteran actor who starred in some of the best classic films of all time, such as *National Velvet, Breakfast at Tiffany's, Requiem for a Heavyweight,* and *Black Stallion*? He died in April 2014 at the age of ninety-three.

You might think that a longtime Hollywood celebrity like Rooney, who appeared in more than three hundred films and TV shows, who won Golden Globes and was honored with an Academy Award, would have been worth millions. Unfortunately, Rooney made and lost millions over his career, struggled with alcoholism and addiction, and married and divorced eight times. He was also a victim of elder financial abuse. At the time of his death, he was reportedly worth $18,000.[2]

While it's true that Rooney had lifelong troubles with finances, what surely made his final years more difficult was the fact that he had so many stepchildren and ex-wives, many of whom did not get along with each other.

His complicated family situation made him especially vulnerable to being financially exploited, because he had long since turned over the day-to-day handling of his finances and daily care to others.

Just one year after celebrating his ninetieth birthday at a star-studded gala at the Loew's Regency Hotel in New York with Donald Trump, Tony Bennett, and Regis Philbin, Rooney's life took an unexpected and unwelcome turn. On February 14, 2011, Michael Augustine, an attorney who had been appointed temporary conservator for the ailing actor, filed a lawsuit against Rooney's stepson Christopher Aber and his wife, Christina. Christopher was the son of Rooney's most recent wife, Janice Rooney, from a previous marriage.

That lawsuit alleged that Rooney had been physically and emotionally abused for years, while being deprived of food and medications by his caregivers. Moreover, the lawsuit claimed—among other things—that his stepson had squandered millions of Rooney's savings and failed to pay the mortgage on his house for more than five months.

Rooney "believes that Christopher Aber had coerced him into signing documents which resulted in financial detriment," asserted court filings at the time, and he "believes that his assets have been depleted by Christopher Aber and he is fearful that because [he] is gaining steps to regain control over his assets, Christopher Aber will do him bodily harm."[3]

As befits a man of his pugnacious reputation, the legendary actor did not go down without a fight. On March 2, 2011, Rooney testified before a special Senate committee formed to consider legislation to curb abuses of senior citizens. "I felt trapped, scared, used and frustrated," Rooney told the senators. "My money was taken and misused. When I asked for information, I was told that I couldn't have any of my own information. I was literally left powerless. But above all, when a man feels helpless, it's terrible."

And in words that will surely be long remembered, Rooney wisely observed, "If elder abuse happened to me, Mickey Rooney, it can happen to anyone."

In October 2013, Rooney's court-appointed conservator agreed to a $2.8 million stipulated judgment (reached by both parties with the judge's sanction). That settled the case between the exploited elderly actor's conservator and Christopher and Christina Aber.

Although Rooney's finances stabilized once a conservator took over, he never lived long enough to recoup any of that money. His stepson and stepson's wife filed for bankruptcy, and in July 2015, their insurance company refused to cover the judgment.

Unfortunately, the story doesn't end there, either. In October 2017, Rooney's estranged widow, Janice, filed a lawsuit against her son Mark Aber, the younger brother of Christopher Aber, and Mark's wife, Charlene. She claimed that they were responsible for abusing Mickey and that they had formed a "bogus management company" that influenced Mickey to sign a contract giving them 15 percent of Mickey's earnings.[4]

Yes, the Rooney family feud will eventually come to an end, but the damage has already been inflicted, and no one is going to come out of it for the better. Mickey was right— if it can happen to him, it can happen to anyone.

The lesson from the Mickey Rooney case seems clear to me: When communication between family members breaks down, everyone suffers. Elders become much more vulnerable to cons and caretaker abuse when family members turn a blind eye. How much of Mickey Rooney's sad end could have been avoided is anyone's guess, but surely the family should have rallied around the patriarch to make his final years happier.

For all his faults as a human being—and like all of us, Mickey Rooney had plenty of them—surely he deserved a happier ending.

The Butler Really Did Do It: The Doris Duke Case

If you need yet another example that being rich and famous does not insulate someone from the threat of cons and malicious caretakers, consider what happened to the billionaire heiress Doris Duke.

Duke died in 1993 at the age of eighty-one, so maybe you don't remember who she is, but she was the heiress to the James Duke tobacco fortune, $40 million of which was donated in 1924 to what was then called Trinity College. Today we know it as Duke University, one of the top-ranked and most prestigious universities in the world.

James Duke may have left Trinity College $40 million, but he left his twelve-year-old daughter the lion's share of his fortune, which at the time was nearly $100 million.

Despite a luxurious, extravagant lifestyle that included homes in five places (including Hawaii, Beverly Hills, and Park Avenue) and a full-time staff of two hundred, Duke watched her inheritance grow. By the time she was in her seventies, she had a net worth of more than a billion dollars. Fortunately, she could not spend her money fast enough, so she ultimately decided to set up the Doris Duke Charitable Foundation to support environmental causes and fight the abuse of children and animals.

As with many cases of elder financial abuse, the catalyst for Doris Duke's case came through an association with dubious people. Divorced and with no close family of her own, Duke befriended a young woman named Chandi who claimed to be the reincarnation of Duke's deceased baby girl, who, when Duke was twenty-seven, died twenty-fours after being born prematurely. Chandi and her boyfriend, who served as Duke's bodyguard, ingratiated themselves into her life and were richly rewarded. Duke gave Chandi a million-dollar home in Hawaii, among many other lavish gifts. And it was Chandi who introduced Duke to a man named Bernard Lafferty, who went on to serve as Duke's butler for six years and eventually became her closest friend and confidante.[5]

The story of Doris Duke and Bernard Lafferty was made into a wonderful 2006 movie called *Bernard and Doris* starring Susan Sarandon as Duke and Ralph Fiennes as Lafferty. While we could never believe that Ralph Fiennes would ever be guilty of elder financial abuse, the real Bernard Lafferty was far less credible.

In 1990, when Duke was seventy-eight, she became mysteriously ill at her home in Hawaii. Lafferty persuaded her that Chandi and her boyfriend were conspiring against her. They moved back to Beverly Hills, where Duke became clinically depressed and turned over the management of her life and affairs to Lafferty. Just six months before she died, she installed Lafferty as the executor of her will and put him in charge of the Doris Duke Foundation, all of which amounted to a gift of more than $10 million. For months, Duke was in and out of hospitals, taking multiple painkillers, and isolated from everyone except Lafferty. One day, after she started choking, Lafferty reportedly refused to call an ambulance. She died on October 28, 1993, after many painful months of suffering.[6]

The former executor of Duke's estate, her doctor, immediately contested the validity of Duke's new will and claimed that Lafferty had used undue influence to put himself in charge. The litigation lasted for three years, involved forty lawyers, and ultimately consumed $10 million in legal fees, but Lafferty took a payout, renounced his seat on the Doris Duke Charitable Foundation board, and stepped down as executor.[7]

No charges were ever filed against Lafferty, but his life did not end happily. After Duke's death, he lived at her Bel Air estate until November 1996, at which point he died as a result of alcohol and drug abuse.

So, yes, in this case, the butler did do it—but he did not get away with it.

Today, the Doris Duke Charitable Foundation is a thriving nonprofit with nearly $2 billion in assets and supports many worthy causes around the world.

Acknowledgments

Alzheimer's, Widowed Stepmothers & Estate Crimes is dedicated to my children and grandchildren. This dedication reflects the joy that my spouse, Lisa, and I share as grandparents. The words of Proverbs 17:6 ring particularly true for us: "Grandchildren are the crown of the aged, and the glory of children is their parents."

Among several people indispensable to this book, my son, Mark Hackard, comes first. He is an untiring helper, the editor of some four hundred videos that we have produced, and a continuing reminder that our job is to help people who are feeling the pain of estate, trust, and elder financial abuse challenges.

I also owe particular thanks to J.P. Mark. He is a source of inspiration and encouragement—and the research that made this book possible. I also give great credit to John Long, who manages the business side of Hackard Law, my law firm. Because of John's management I am able to practice law in a fulfilling manner, write books, and engage the media in spreading the message of elder financial abuse awareness.

The great Adam Rosen of AMR Editorial was my editor for *The Wolf at the Door: Undue Influence and Elder Financial Abuse*, as he is for *Alzheimer's, Widowed Stepmothers & Estate Crimes*. I can always depend on Adam to take what I have written and make it better, clearer, and more compelling.

Finally, I want to give thanks to my family, my colleagues, and my clients. Those who seek our assistance are the genesis for many of the insights that I'm privileged to share. I'm grateful to all of those who have graciously contributed to our effort to bring attention to the plight of elders vulnerable to financial exploitation and abuse.

Notes

PREFACE

1. "2015 Alzheimer's disease facts and figures," *Alzheimer's & Dementia: The Journal of the Alzheimer's Association* 11, no. 3 (March 2015): 332–384, https://www.alzheimersanddementia.com/article/S1552-5260(15)00058-8/fulltext.

INTRODUCTION

1. Alex Haley, "What *Roots* Means to Me," *Reader's Digest*, May 1977.

CHAPTER 1

1. "Alzheimer's Diagnosis Rarely Disclosed to Patients," Alzheimers.net, accessed September 22, 2018, https://www.alzheimers.net/4-13-15-alzheimers-diagnosis-rarely-disclosed/.
2. Felice J. Freyer, "A landmark law hopes to improve Alzheimer's care in Mass.," *Boston Globe*, August 13, 2018, accessed September 21, 2018, https://www.bostonglobe.com/metro/2018/08/12/new-mass-law-aims-improve-alzheimer-care/qTtWWD1TrqOoENrRyEMXHI/story.htmlr.
3. "Abuse," Alzheimer's Association, accessed September 22, 2018, https://www.alz.org/help-support/caregiving/safety/abuse.
4. See Michael Hackard, *The Wolf at the Door: Undue Influence and Elder Financial Abuse* (Mather, CA: Hackard Global Media, 2017).
5. "Managing Money Problems in Alzheimer's Disease," National Institute on Aging, accessed September 22, 2018, https://www.nia.nih.gov/health/managing-money-problems-alzheimers-disease.

CHAPTER 2

1. Alison Boshoff, "The worst father in the world? Tony Curtis neglected his children. Now they're having to sue for a share of his £37million fortune," *Daily Mail*, March 31, 2011, accessed September 22, 2018, http://www.dailymail.co.uk/tvshowbiz/article-1372106/Tony-Curtis-worst-father-world-Children-sue-share-37million-fortune.html.
2. "Estate of Tony Curtis Auction Catalog: Property from the Estate of Tony Curtis," Julien's Auctions, September 17, 2011, accessed September 22, 2018, http://www.juliensauctions.com/shop/index.php?l=product_detail&p=90.

3. https://www.hackardlaw.com/blog/2014/12/tony-curtis-estate-dispute.shtml

4. Mike Hackard, "The Curious Case of Tony Curtis," Hackard Law blog, December 17, 2014, accessed September 22, 2018, https://www.hackardlaw.com/blog/2014/12 /tony-curtis-estate-dispute.shtml.

5. Danielle and Andy Mayoras, "Tony Curtis' Kids Say He Was the Victim of Undue Influence," Forbes.com, September 19, 2011, accessed September 22, 2018, https://www.forbes.com/sites/trialandheirs/2011/09/19/tony-curtis-kids-say-he-was -the-victim-of-undue-influence/#47a1b181444f.

6. "Tony Curtis's Daughter Speaks Out About Disinheritance," InsideEdition.com, September 12, 2011, accessed September 22, 2018, https://www.insideedition.com /headlines/3025-tony-curtiss-daughter-speaks-out-about-disinheritance.

7. Eric Alt, "Tony Curtis Wrote His Children Out of His Will," NBCSanDiego.com, March 9, 2011, accessed September 22, 2018, https://www.nbcsandiego.com /entertainment/celebrity/Tony-Curtis-Disowned-His-Children-Before-His-Death- 117658213.html.

8. "2018 California Rules of Court," Judicial Council of California, accessed September 22, 2018, http://www.courts.ca.gov/cms/rules/index.cfm?title=seven&linkid=rule7 _703.

9. Cal. BPC § 6147, https://leginfo.legislature.ca.gov/faces/codes_displaySection .xhtml?sectionNum=6147.&lawCode=BPC.

CHAPTER 3

1. Frank J. Prial, "After Settling Estate, Johnson Lawyers Still Battling," *New York Times*, May 7, 1987, accessed September 22, 2018, https://www.nytimes.com /1987/05/07/nyregion/after-settling-estate-johnson-lawyers-still-battling.html.

2. Ibid.

3. Mike Hackard, "Elder Financial Abuse in California | Vulnerabilities," Hackard Law blog, December 1, 2016, accessed September 22, 2018, https://www.hackardlaw.com /blog/2016/12/elder-financial-abuse-in-ca-vulnerabilities.shtml.

4. "How Courts Work," American Bar Association, December 2, 2013, accessed November 20, 2018, https://www.americanbar.org/groups/public_education/resources /law_related_education_network/how_courts_work/discovery/.

5. Mike Hackard, "Countering Undue Influence | CA Estate Litigation," Hackard Law blog, December 1, 2016, accessed September 22, 2018, https://www.hackardlaw.com /blog/2016/12/countering-undue-influence-ca-estate-litigation.shtml.

6. "Elder Abuse Laws (Civil - Private Actions)," State of California Department of Justice, accessed September 22, 2018, https://oag.ca.gov/bmfea/laws/private_elder.

CHAPTER 4

1. John Lennon and Yoko Ono, "Beautiful Boy (Darling Boy)," track 7 on *Double Fantasy*, Geffen Records, 1980, 33⅓ rpm.

2. Barbranda Lumpkins Walls, "Haven't Done a Will Yet?" AARP.org, accessed November 27, 2018, https://www.aarp.org/money/investing/info-2017/half-of-adults-do- not-have-wills.html.

3. Cal. Prob. Code § 810, http://leginfo.legislature.ca.gov/faces/codes_displaySection .xhtml?sectionNum=810.&lawCode=PROB.

4. Cal. Prob. Code § 812, http://leginfo.legislature.ca.gov/faces/codes_displaySection .xhtml?sectionNum=812.&lawCode=PROB.

5. See the website of the American Association for Geriatric Psychiatry, https://www .aagponline.org/.

6. Cal. Evid. Code § 957, http://leginfo.legislature.ca.gov/faces/codes_displaySection .xhtml?sectionNum=957.&lawCode=EVID.

7. Cal. Welf. & Inst. Code § 15610.70, http://leginfo.legislature.ca.gov/faces /codes_displaySection.xhtml?sectionNum=15610.70&lawCode=WIC.

8. Ibid.

9. Hal Espen, "The Sad, Strange Family Battle Over Radio Legend Casey Kasem," *Hollywood Reporter*, February 14, 2014, accessed November 20, 2018, https://www .hollwoodreporter.com/news/casey-kasem-sad-strange-family-678902.

10. "Casey Kasem: His Mind Is Gone," TMZ.com, November 17, 2013, accessed November 20, 2018, http://www.tmz.com/2013/10/17/casey-kasem-conservatorship -mental-state-jean/.

11. Charles Dickens, *A Christmas Carol in Prose, Being a Ghost Story of Christmas* (London: Chapman and Hall, 1843).

CHAPTER 5

1. Dave Boucher, "Fred Thompson's sons sue late senator's wife in estate fight," *Tennessean*, August 13, 2016, accessed September 22, 2018, http://www.tennessean.com /story/news/2016/08/03/fred-thompsons-sons-sue-late-senators-wife-estate-fight /88000110/.

2. Dave Boucher, "Fred Thompson's wife: Adult sons never major part of will," *Tennessean*, August 8, 2016, accessed November 8, 2018, https://www.tennessean.com /story/news/2016/08/08/fred-thompsons-wife-adult-sons-never-part/88316082/.

3. Stacey Barchenger, "Dispute over Sen. Fred Thompson's estate ends," *Tennessean*, August 13, 2016, accessed September 22, 2018, https://www.tennessean.com /story/news/2017/04/03/dispute-over-sen-fred-thompsons-estate-ends/99598332/.

4. Francesca Bacardi, "Alan Thicke's family still trading barbs over estate," *New York Post*, June 13, 2018, accessed November 8, 2018, https://pagesix.com/2018/06/13 /alan-thickes-family-still-trading-barbs-over-estate/.

5. Natalie Stone, "Robin Thicke & His Father Alan's Widow Celebrate Their Love For Late Actor After Judge Throws Out Singer's Lawsuit," *People*, September 24, 2017, accessed November 8, 2018, https://people.com/tv/alan-thicke-widow-lawsuit -stepsons-thrown-out/.

6. Mike Hackard, "The Widowed Stepmother | Big Trust and Estate Fights," Hackard Law blog, November 10, 2015, accessed September 22, 2018, https://www .hackardlaw.com/blog/2015/11/stepmother-trust-estate-fights-ahead.shtml.

7. Larry Copeland, "Life expectancy in the USA hits a record high," *USA Today*, October 9, 2014, accessed September 23, 2018, https://www.usatoday.com/story/news /nation/2014/10/08/us-life-expectancy-hits-record-high/16874039/.

8. Russell Heimlich, "Baby Boomers Retire," Fact Tank: News in the Numbers, Pew Research Center, November 29, 2010, accessed September 22, 2018, http://www.pewresearch.org/fact-tank/2010/12/29/baby-boomers-retire/.

9. María M. Corrada, Ron Brookmeyer, Annlia Paganini-Hill, Daniel Berlau, and Claudia H. Kawas, "Dementia Incidence Continues to Increase with Age in the Oldest Old: The 90+ Study," *Annals of Neurology* 67, no. 1 (2010): 114–21, https://www.ncbi.nlm.nih.gov/pmc/articles/PMC3385995/.

10. Wednesday Martin, "Guess Who Has the Power in a Remarriage with Children?" *Psychology Today*, October 7, 2009, accessed November 8, 2018, https://www.psychologytoday.com/us/blog/stepmonster/200910/guess-who-has-the-power-in-re-marriage-children.

11. Brian O'Connell, "My Stepmother Stole My Inheritance," *TheStreet*, February 8, 2018, accessed September 23, 2018, https://www.thestreet.com/story/14480922/1/my-stepmother-stole-my-inheritance.html.

12. Abraham Lincoln, "First Inaugural Address," speech, March 4, 1861, "First Inaugural Address of Abraham Lincoln," The Avalon Project, Lillian Goldman Law Library, accessed September 23, 2018, http://avalon.law.yale.edu/19th_century/lincoln1.asp.

13. Abraham Lincoln, "Second Inaugural Address," speech, March 4, 1866, "Second Inaugural Address of Abraham Lincoln," The Avalon Project, Lillian Goldman Law Library, accessed September 23, 2018, http://avalon.law.yale.edu/19th_century/lincoln2.asp.

CHAPTER 6

1. Cal. Prob. Code § 8420, http://leginfo.legislature.ca.gov/faces/codes_displaySection.xhtml?sectionNum=8420.&lawCode=PROB.

2. "Sobering Facts: Drunk Driving in California," Centers for Disease Control and Prevention, 2014, accessed September 22, 2018, https://www.cdc.gov/motorvehiclesafety/pdf/impaired_driving/drunk_driving_in_ca.pdf.

3. "2014 Annual Report of the California DUI Management Information System," State of California Department of Motor Vehicles, accessed September 23, 2018, https://www.dmv.ca.gov/portal/wcm/connect/ea06d0a4-a73f-4b2d-b6f1-257029275629/S5-246.pdf?MOD=AJPERES&CONVERT_TO=url&CACHEID=ea06d0a4-a73f-4b2d-b6f1-257029275629.

4. "California Drug Abuse Statistics," Duffys Napa Valley Rehab, November 30, 2013, accessed September 23, http://visual.ly/california-drug-abuse-statistics.

5. Mike Hackard, "Unfair Trust Distributions: Can You Sue in Sacramento Probate Court?" Hackard Law blog, April 5, 2016, accessed September 22, 2018, https://www.hackardlaw.com/blog/2016/04/unfair-trust-distributions-can-you-sue-in-sacramento-probate-court.shtml.

6. Mike Hackard, "Trustee Accountability | When Requests for an Accounting Fail," Hackard Law blog, September 23, 2016, accessed September 22, 2018, https://www.hackardlaw.com/blog/2016/09/trustee-accountability-when-requests-for-an-acounting-fail.shtml.

7. Mike Hackard, "Contempt of Court Against Former Trustees | Sacramento, California," Hackard Law blog, August 29, 2016, accessed September 22, 2018, https://www.hackardlaw.com/blog/2016/08/contempt-of-court-against-former-trustees-sacramento-california.shtml.
8. "Trustee's Duty to Inform Beneficiaries: Clarification and Expansion," Legislative Proposal (T&E-2009-09), State Bar of California, June 14, 2008, accessed September 22, 2018, http://www.calbar.ca.gov/LinkClick.aspx?fileticket=WI83wtUp1fc%3D&tabid=752.
9. Nathan Pastor, "The Trust Litigator's Arsenal," Contra Costa Lawyer Online, December 1, 2015, accessed September 23, 2018, http://cclawyer.cccba.org/2015/12/the-trust-litigators-arsenal/.
10. "2016 Court Statistics Report: Statewide Caseload Trends, 2005–2006 Through 2014–2015," Judicial Council of California, 2016, accessed September 23, 2018, http://www.courts.ca.gov/documents/2016-Court-Statistics-Report.pdf.
11. "Probate Court: Living Trusts," Superior Court of California, County of Alameda website, accessed September 23, 2018, http://www.alameda.courts.ca.gov/Pages.aspx/Living-Trusts-and-Estate-Planning.
12. Mike Hackard, "Guarding Trust Beneficiary Rights | Los Angeles," Hackard Law blog, June 21, 2017, accessed September 23, 2018, https://www.hackardlaw.com/blog/2017/06/guarding-trust-beneficiary-rights-los-angeles.shtml.
13. *Fiduciary Trust International of California v. Klein*, 9 Cal. App. 5th 1184 (2017), https://cases.justia.com/california/court-of-appeal/2017-a144558.pdf?ts=1490119228.
14. Cal. Evid. Code § 954, http://leginfo.legislature.ca.gov/faces/codes_displaySection.xhtml?lawCode=EVID&sectionNum=954.
15. "Probate Trusts," Superior Court of California, County of Santa Clara website, accessed September 23, 2018, http://www.scscourt.org/self_help/probate/property/probate_trusts.shtml.
16. *Moeller v. Superior Court (Sanwa Bank)*, 16 Cal.4th 1124, 947 P.2d 279 (1997), https://law.justia.com/cases/california/supreme-court/4th/16/1124.html.
17. Mike Hackard, "Los Angeles Trust Litigation Attorney | Asking the Right Questions," Hackard Law blog, May 8, 2017, accessed September 23, 2018, https://www.hackardlaw.com/blog/2017/05/los-angeles-trust-litigation-attorney-asking-the-right-questions.shtml.
18. Mike Hackard, "CA Trust Litigation | Are You Prepared & Protected?" Hackard Law blog, March 22, 2017, accessed September 23, 2018, https://www.hackardlaw.com/blog/2017/03/trust-litigation-making-sure-youre-prepared-protected.shtml.

CHAPTER 7

1. Mike Hackard, "Do-It-Yourself Estate Law," Hackard Law blog, May 21, 2015, accessed September 23, 2018, https://www.hackardlaw.com/blog/2015/05/do-it-yourself-estate-law.shtml.
2. Mike Hackard, "Trying to Hide the Will? We'll See About That," Hackard Law blog, September 17, 2015, accessed September 23, 2018, https://www.hackardlaw.com/blog/2015/09/trying-to-hide-a-will-well-see-about-that.shtml.

CHAPTER 8

1. Kelly Phillips Erb, "17 Famous People Who Died Without a Will," Forbes.com, April 27, 2016, accessed September 23, 2018, https://www.forbes.com/sites /kellyphillipserb/2016/04/27/17-famous-people-who-died-without-a-will/.

2. Daniel Kreps, "Prince Estate: Sister, Five Half-Siblings Named Heirs," *Rolling Stone*, May 20, 2017, accessed September 22, 2018, http://www.rollingstone.com /music/news/prince-estate-sister-five-half-siblings-named-heirs-w483355.

3. Bob Egelko, "Botched wills can be fixed after death, state high court says," *San Francisco Chronicle*, July 28, 2015, accessed September 22, 2018, http://www.sfgate .com/news/article/Botched-wills-can-be-fixed-after-death-state-6411092.php.

4. "Docket NO. S199435: Estate of Duke," Robert Crown Law Library, Stanford Law School, accessed November 9, 2018, https://scocal.stanford.edu/opinion/estate-duke -34429.

5. Plutarch, *Lives of the Noble Grecians and Romans,* trans. John Dryden, ed. A. H. Clough, hosted by eBooks@Adelaide, University of Adelaide, December 17, 2014, accessed September 23, 2018, https://ebooks.adelaide.edu.au/p/plutarch/lives/.

6. Ibid.

7. "REPORTS OF CASES DECIDED BY FRANCIS BACON, BARON VERULAM, VISCOUNT ST. ALBANS, LORD CHANCELLOR OF ENGLAND," National Guardianship Association, accessed November 12, 2018, http://www.guardianship.org /IRL/Resources/Handouts/Undue%20Influence_Bacon%20Case.pdf.

8. Welf. & Inst. Code § 15610.70, http://leginfo.legislature.ca.gov/faces/codes _displaySection.xhtml?sectionNum=15610.70&lawCode=WIC.

9. Cal. Prob. Codes § 8870–8873, http://leginfo.legislature.ca.gov/faces/codes_display Section.xhtml?sectionNum=8870.&lawCode=PROB; http://leginfo.legislature.ca.gov /faces/codes_displaySection.xhtml?sectionNum=8871.&lawCode=PROB; http://leginfo.legislature.ca.gov/faces/codes_displaySection.xhtml?sectionNum=8872 .&lawCode=PROB; http://leginfo.legislature.ca.gov/faces/codes_displaySection.xhtml ?sectionNum=8873.&lawCode=PROB.

10. "Missing Records," The U.S. National Archives and Record Administration, accessed September 23, 2018, http://www.archives.gov/research/recover/missing -documents.html.

11. Hackard, "Trying to Hide the Will? We'll See About That."

12. Cal. Prob. Code § 6124, http://leginfo.legislature.ca.gov/faces/codes_displaySec- tion.xhtml?sectionNum=6124.&lawCode=PROB.

13. Cal. Prob. Code § 8223, http://leginfo.legislature.ca.gov/faces/codes_displaySec- tion.xhtml?sectionNum=8223.&lawCode=PROB.

14. Cal. Prob. Code § 21311, https://leginfo.legislature.ca.gov/faces/codes _displaySection.xhtml?lawCode=PROB&sectionNum=21311.

15. Jeffrey M. Jones, "Majority in U.S. Do Not Have a Will," Gallup poll, May 18, 2016, accessed November 9, 2018, https://news.gallup.com/poll/191651/majority-not .aspx.

CHAPTER 9

1. Mark Glover, "Do you have money waiting? Online database of unclaimed safe deposit boxes expands," *Sacramento Bee*, April 6, 2017, accessed September 23, 2018, https://www.sacbee.com/news/business/article143116519.html.

2. "Bank Of America Let Conwoman Steal My Dead Aunt's Identity And Rob Her Safe Deposit Box," Consumerist.com, April 23, 2017, accessed September 23, 2018, https://consumerist.com/2007/04/23/bank-of-america-let-conwoman-steal-my-dead-aunts-identity-and-rob-her-safe-deposit-box/.

3. Mike Hackard, "CA Trustee's Bad Ideas | Hiding the Trust from Beneficiaries," Hackard Law blog, September 26, 2017, accessed September 23, 2018, https://www.hackardlaw.com/blog/2017/09/ca-trustees-bad-ideas-hiding-the-trust-from-beneficiaries.shtml.

4. Michael Thrasher, "Safe Deposit Boxes: Your Valuables Aren't Actually Insured or Safe," ValuePenguin, April 25, 2015, accessed September 23, 2018, https://www.valuepenguin.com/2015/04/safe-deposit-boxes-your-valuables-arent-actually-insured-or-safe.

5. Cal. Prob. Code § 8223, https://leginfo.legislature.ca.gov/faces/codes_displaySection.xhtml?lawCode=PROB&sectionNum=331.

CHAPTER 10

1. Michael P. Mayko, "Lawyer sentenced to prison for theft from dead woman's estate," *Connecticut Post*, January 14, 2016, accessed October 3, 2018, https://www.ctpost.com/news/article/Lawyer-faces-jail-in-theft-from-dead-woman-s-6755737.php.

2. "The Crime of the 21st Century: Elder Financial Abuse," *Probate & Property Magazine* 28, no. 04 (July–August 2014), https://www.americanbar.org/publications/probate_property_magazine_2012/2014/july_august_2014/2014_aba_rpte_pp_v28_4_article_lewis_elder_financial_abuse.html.

3. Welf. & Inst. Code § 15630, https://leginfo.legislature.ca.gov/faces/codes_displaySection.xhtml?lawCode=WIC&sectionNum=15630.

CHAPTER 11

1. "Planning Ahead for Legal Matters," Alzheimer's Association, accessed September 23, 2018, https://www.alz.org/help-support/caregiving/financial-legal-planning/planning-ahead-for-legal-matters.

2. Gary Baum and Scott Feinberg, "Tears and Terror: The Disturbing Final Years of Mickey Rooney," *The Hollywood Reporter*, October 21, 2015, accessed October 4, 2018, https://www.hollywoodreporter.com/features/mickey-rooneys-final-years-833325.

3. Maria Elena Fernandez, "Mickey Rooney's stepson ordered to turn over all of the actor's ID cards," *Los Angeles Times*, February 25, 2011, accessed September 22, 2018, http://articles.latimes.com/2011/feb/25/entertainment/la-et-rooney-20110225.

4. Donna Smith, "Actor Mickey Rooney tells Congress abuse," Reuters, March 2, 2011, accessed October 8, 2018, https://www.reuters.com/article/us-mickeyrooney /actor-mickey-rooney-tells-congress-of-abuse-idUSTRE7217BX20110302.

5. Patricia Brennan, "Doris Duke: The Curse of Money," *Washington Post*, February 21, 1999, accessed October 8, 2018, https://www.washingtonpost.com/archive /lifestyle/tv/1999/02/21/doris-duke-the-curse-of-money/4e53cdae-e239-4a45-8dd3 -d2c5e90b4972/.

6. "Doris Duke," Biography.com, accessed June 15, 2018, https://www.biography.com /people/doris-duke-9542083.

7. "Doris Duke - Billionaire Heiress And Victim Of Elder Abuse," Talbot Law Group, P.C. blog, March 26, 2016, accessed September 23, 2018, https://www .matthewbtalbot.com/blog/2015/11/4/doridukeelderabuse.

Index

AARP, 41

addiction, 50, 67–68, 81–82

advance health care directives, 98

Alzheimer's disease, 5, 119

    diagnosis of, 10–12, 14–15

    mediation and, 13

    statistics on, 4, 11, 59–60

American Bar Association, 111

attorney-client privilege, 44, 73, 114

blended families, 5, 26–28, 75–85

    growth of, 4, 26

    personalities in, 79–83

    statistics on, 4, 27, 59–61, 76

    suggestions for, 61–64, 83–85

    See also stepmothers

Bono, Sonny, 87

burden of proof, 9, 23, 42–43

California Appellate Court, 73

California Court of Appeals, 72–73

California Evidence Code, 44

California Probate Code, 71, 92, 94, 95–96, 102, 112

California State Controller's Office, 100

California Superior Court, 17, 107

California Supreme Court, 88–89

California Welfare and Institutions Code, 45–46

Cantil-Sakauye, Tani, 88

capacity. *See* mental capacity

caretakers, 30, 96, 112, 119–26

children, familial rights and, 25–26

civil cases

    burden of proof and, 9

    deadlines, 16, 32

    elder financial abuse and, 112–14

    juries and, 9, 17, 107, 113

    statistics on, 12

Clark, Peter, 110–11

cognitive decline, 6–17

    accidental disinheritance and, 24–26

diagnosis of, 10

protection and, 13–15

See also Alzheimer's disease; dementia; Lewy Body Dementia

community property, 25–26

confidentiality, 10, 44, 73, 114

conflict management, 84–85

contingency fees, 8–9, 22–23, 114

creditors, 70, 116

Curtis, Tony, 18–21, 28, 58

deadlines, 16–17, 32, 105

dementia, 4, 10–12, 46–49, 59–60, 119

dependency, 50

discovery process, 32–33

disinheritance, 18–28

accidental, 24–26

contesting, 6–10, 15–17, 23–24

litigation fees, 21–23

reasons for, 11–12, 20–21

doctor-patient confidentiality, 10

Duke, Doris, 123–26

Duke, Irving, 88

durable power of attorney, 98

Elder Abuse and Dependent Adult Civil Protection Act, 112–13

elder financial abuse, 6–10, 108–18

defined, 32

evidence of, 115–16

litigating, 112–14

preventing, 14–15, 116–18

estate crimes

fraud and, 14, 108–14

inheritance and, 5

safe deposit boxes and, 101

statistics on, 8

See also elder financial abuse; undue influence

estate planning, 40–53

advance health care directives, 9

assumptions about, 49–53

durable power of attorney, 98

failure to plan, 41–43, 49–50

mental capacity and, 42–46

statistics on, 41, 98, 100

See also trusts/trustees; wills

estate taxes, 51–52

evidence, 32–36, 44

executor, defined, 66

"ex parte," 72

expert witnesses, 11, 43

familial relationships, rights and, 25–26

FBI, 7, 8, 111

fees
    contingency, 8–9, 22–23, 114
    disinheritance litigation and,
        21–23
    mediation, 12–13
    mental capacity cases and, 9–10
    responsibility for, 9
Fiduciary Trust International of
    California v. Klein, 72–74
Form 706 (estate taxes), 51–52
fraud, 14, 108–18

HackardLaw.com, 49

incapacity. *See* mental capacity
inheritance, evolution of, 1–5
inheritance, lost, 6–17
intestacy laws, 86–87
irrevocable/revocable trusts, 16,
    70, 72, 117

Johnson, Robert Wood, 29–31
Judicial Council of California, 72
juries, 9, 17, 31, 107, 113

Kasem, Casey, 46–49
Klein, Fiduciary Trust International
    of California v., 72–74

legal representation, basis for, 7–10
letters of testamentary, 103
Lewis, Jerry Lee, 77–78, 79
Lewy Body Dementia, 10, 47
Lincoln, Abraham, 87
litigation, 29–39
    approaches to, 15–17
    burden of proof, 9, 23, 42–43
    deadlines, 16–17, 32, 105
    discovery process, 32–36
    economic justification for, 8–10
    elder financial abuse, 112–14
    interview process, 36–39
    litigator profiles, 79–83
    managing conflict, 84–85
    personalities, 79–83
    risks/rewards of, 38–39
    safe deposit boxes, 100–107
    standard questions, 37–38
    See also civil cases; fees; juries;
        probate court; timelines;
        specific case
living trusts, 41, 66, 72, 92
Lobkowicz, William, 3
lost inheritance, 6–17

mediation, 12–13, 84–85
mental capacity, 6–17
    defined, 43

estate planning and, 42–46

legal fees and, 9–10

test to determine, 42–43

no-contact lists, 117–18

no contest clauses, 96–97

O'Connell, Brian, 61

predeceased spouses, familial
rights and, 26

Prince (singer), 87

probate code, 71, 92, 94, 95–96,
102, 112

probate court

approaches, 15–17

executors and, 66

statistics on, 72

trustees and, 69–70

revocable/irrevocable trusts, 16,
70, 72, 117

Rooney, Mickey, 121–23

safes/safe deposit boxes, 100–107

separate property, 25–26

spousal rights, 25–26

Stepfamily Foundation, 4

stepmothers, 4–5, 54–64

personalities of, 79–80

statistics on, 27, 59–61

suggestions for, 61–64

Strong, Miriam, 110–11

substance abuse, 50, 67–68, 81–82

survivorship, 25–26

taxes, estate, 51–52

TheStreet, 61

Thicke, Alan, 56–57, 58

Thompson, Fred, 54–56, 58

timelines

filing deadlines, 16–17, 32, 105

preparing, 16–17, 37, 70, 106,
108–10

trusts/trustees, 65–74

challenging, 68–69, 95–97

deadlines, 16

defined, 66, 72

duties of, 66, 70–71

living trusts, 41, 66, 72, 92

removing trustees, 68–72

revocable/irrevocable, 16, 70, 72,
117

substance abuse and, 67–68, 81–

undue influence

defined, 27, 45–46, 91

fraud and, 14

proving, 7–8, 23–24

wills and, 88–91

vulnerability, 45–46

wills, 86–99

    challenging, 95–97

    errors in, 88–89

hiding of, 91–93

importance of, 41–43, 49–50

intestacy laws, 86–87

lost, 93–95

no contest clauses, 96–97

statistics on, 41, 98

undue influence and, 88–91

Winehouse, Amy, 87

About the Author

MICHAEL HACKARD is the founder of Hackard Law, a California law firm that focuses on estate and trust litigation. Over his forty-plus-year career, he has helped many victims of elder financial abuse and disinheritance, including trust beneficiaries, disinherited heirs, and relatives of family members. His 2017 book on elder financial abuse, *The Wolf at the Door*, garnered press from many national outlets.

Mike has an "AV Rating" from Martindale-Hubbell® Peer Review, signifying the highest level of professional excellence. He has been interviewed regularly by local and national media, including the *Wall Street Journal*, MarketWatch, MSN Money, C-SPAN, and Fox News, and has testified before the House of Representatives.

Mike received his JD from the McGeorge School of Law and has been a member of the California Bar Association since 1976. He lives in Sacramento, California, and can be contacted at hackard@hackardlaw.com.

To learn more about Mike and about inheritance-related issues, please visit www.hackardlaw.com.

Please send all media or publicity inquiries to Mark Hackard at mark.hackard@hackardlaw.com.

CPSIA information can be obtained
at www.ICGtesting.com
Printed in the USA
FSHW010747220619
59295FS